THE INNER DIMENSION

MOVING INTO FULLNESS

THE INNER DIMENSION

by
Mark J. Chironna

Destiny Image Publishers
P.O. Box 351
Shippensburg, Pa. U.S.A. 17257

"Speaking to the Purposes of God for this Generation"

Printed in the United States of America
ISBN: 0-914903-24-1
For worldwide distribution

Cover by:
Tresa Paul

TABLE OF CONTENTS

1

FROM HEAVEN TO EARTH

"For the Son of Man has come to seek and save THAT WHICH was lost." Both Matthew and Luke record these words for us in their gospel accounts. In the context of Matthew's gospel (18:7-11), Jesus is pronouncing judgement upon those who would cause little ones to stumble and fall in regards to relationship with the Heavenly Father. In Luke's gospel (19:1-10), the statement is made in context with the conversion of Zaccheus, whom Jesus called a child of Abraham. In considering these verses in their context, it becomes apparent that the Lord of glory is not merely interested in the salvation of the individuals concerned, He is interested in the recovery of THAT WHICH was lost. The matter of Incarnation is a matter of RECOVERY. His all-consuming passion was to recover and restore something which was lost ages before His appearing. He Who is the Author and Finisher of the New Creation, was also the Author and Finisher of the first creation. As we come to understand what it was that was lost in the first creation, we can better comprehend the purpose of the New Creation in Christ Jesus.

When moved upon by the tremendous influence of Jesus' ministry, and the power which accompanied His words, the disciples made a request of Him: "Lord, teach us to pray" (Luke 11:1). In response Jesus said, "When you pray, say: Father, hallowed be Thy Name, Thy KINGDOM COME..." In Matthew, we are given a bit more insight; for Matthew records the prayer Jesus taught them using these words: "Our Father, Who art in heaven, Hallowed be Thy Name. Thy Kingdom come, Thy Will be done, on EARTH AS IT IS IN HEAVEN," (Matt. 6:9-10).

I was in a city preaching a series of meetings on this particular text, when in the midst of my sermon while uttering the very words, *"Thy Kingdom come on earth as it is in heaven,"* I saw a mental image that so impacted me that I found myself at a loss for words. Having seen the picture, however, and perceiving the reason for which the Spirit gave it to me, I found myself "speaking beyond" my natural level of understanding, and began to speak what was an oracle of God. After the meeting ended, I set myself to do all the studying I could to see if what I had declared was indeed a God-given revelation. Here then is the picture that I saw, as best as I can describe it:

> I saw a vast wilderness bereft of life and anything living, and as my mouth was saying the words, "Thy Kingdom come on earth as it is in heaven," I saw what resembled my concept of the Shekinah Cloud of God's glory, looking much like a mushroom cloud after an atomic bomb has exploded, and this

cloud came down and began to hover over the wilderness and move across the surface of the earth and begin to create substance where there was no substance. It seemed as though the Lord was impressing my mind with this thought, "This is the picture I want you to comprehend with all its implications when you consider what is implied in asking for My Kingdom to come."

As I went to search out the matter before God in those next few days, I found myself pouring over the passages in Exodus 24 and Exodus 25 when the glory of God descended upon the Mountain of Horeb. I read Exodus 40 and tried as best I could to imagine what it must have been like to be there at the completion of the tabernacle and see the Glory Cloud descend upon the Holy of Holies. I also went to II Chronicles 5 and the dedication of Solomon's temple and saw the amazing similarity between these two passages. Imagine what it must have been like to behold the glory of God in the fullness of that cloud. Yet in my consideration up to that point, I was still hounded by the thought that there was something more to the picture I saw than I apprehended in Exodus 40 or 2 Chronicles 5.

By the gentle nudge of the Spirit, I found myself meditating for days on the first few chapters of Genesis. It was in the book of beginnings that the light of illumination began to break upon my understanding and my heart was opened to see some things that have changed my perspective on my life and my walk with God. It is in the book of origins that the pattern of things to come is unveiled. The things which are revealed there cover symbolically the scope of the history of redemption. Many of the over 3000 symbols in the last book of the Bible, the Revelation given to John, find their first mention in Genesis. The patterns revealed in the original creation account have within them the secret to the heart of God. As we come to understand what takes place in the original creation, there comes an unfolding of the plan, program and purpose of God for time and eternity.

The Bible begins with God and it also ends with God. "In the beginning God," opens to us a door of relationship with the Creator, and "Even so Come Lord Jesus," completes for us the fullest revelation of God there can ever be.

We are told very directly without long and flowery scientific language, that IN the beginning, all things had their origin in God Himself. He created everything there is. God created the heavens and the earth. Included in the heavens was not only the universe with its many galaxies, planets, stars, quasars, and whatever else there may be, but also the heaven of heavens which is the abode of the Almighty. But in the midst of the great expanse known as the heavens, for all the multiplied billions of stars and heavenly spheres that He created, He has taken special interest in the planet called earth, as small and insignificant as it may seem. This tiny planet pales in the light of the stars and planets that hang in the vast skies that surround it. But the Creator took special interest in this planet and moved upon it to create an atmosphere suitable for a man, that He would create, to inhabit and populate. He created man to be His co-regent over the earth, and in cooperation with the Creator Himself, to rule over the works of His hands.

Man was to be the ultimate in the creation of God. Of all that God created man was to be the epitome of His Image. Yet man was created to be governed by a Word totally outside of his limited scope of thinking. Man was to be God-ruled. Man under the government of God was to "Be fruitful, multiply, fill the earth, subdue it and rule over the works of his hands," (Genesis 1:26). In order for man to be ruled by God, there needed to be an ongoing relationship with God. That relationship had to be based on trust and love. God would have it no other way. Through the man He created, God was to have a people, called by His Name as sons and daughters that bore His image on earth, reflecting and mirroring the reality of His eternal heavenly glory.

The tragedy is that man fell when he sinned and fell short of the glory of God. Adam thus forfeited the right to become a partaker of God's glory. In the fullness of time, God did send His Son, who is the express image of His nature to bring man back to the glory of God.

God's the Supreme CAUSE behind every consequence. All things were begun and initiated by God. Therefore to understand what God intended for man in the beginning, we must begin with what He reveals about Himself through His acts of power and His declarations of Who He is. He is the Self-revealing God. All things were created for His pleasure. His supreme delight is to bring us to a full awareness of His Person.

Originally, Eden was to be the place of unlimited pleasure. It was to be the place where God and man would be in union and harmony. It was in Eden where man in his finite form could relate to and touch the Infinite God. It was here in the garden where all things were in the state of existence that perfectly reflected what God's habitation in the Heavens was like. Eden was the habitation of God and man. Man who lived on earth, and God who dwelt in the eternal heaven found a place of UNION, created by Him, where God and man together might dwell. Paradise was paradise because God was there enjoying fellowship with the man He created in His Image.

None of this came into existence by the will of man. This was God's thought and God's intent. God desired to dwell with man in union with him. DeVerne Fromke puts it so well in his book *The Ultimate Intention,* when he very carefully describes that God had an eternal desire for sons, because He is the FATHER. He did not become a FATHER, His very essence has always been that of FATHER. Jesus did not become His Son at the Incarnation, He was always eternally co-existent with the FATHER as His Son. Fromke reminds us that to understand the purpose of God we must begin with that revelation of His Fatherhood, because all things from that perspective have a paternal overshadowing. Out of His Father-heart, He desired sons, who would be nurtured and raised as apprentices under His upbringing to ultimately rule over all the works of His hands as heirs of all His inheritance.

As Father, God wanted to dwell with His sons. He did not desire to abide merely in heaven, He desired to bring heaven down to earth in all its splendor, and in the fullness of His glory and dwell here on earth, being as comfortable on earth as He was in heaven.

In these days of transition, the Spirit of the Lord is bringing a fresh emphasis on certain truths that have been overlooked or neglected. We have been held in paralysis as the people of God by a gospel of refined legalism that has as its ultimate goal getting man to heaven. There has been a humanistic emphasis in much of the preaching of the "hell or heaven" gospel. The implications being that if you abide by certain rules you will keep yourself from going to hell and work your way into heaven. Tragically, it has produced a spirit of Pharisaism that is fired by the very flames of hell. Never has there been such a judgmentalism in the Church, which has evaluated people and the level of their commitment to God by how well they perform up to the standards of a select few who claim to be the faithful remnant that alone have the truth.

Men who knowingly twist prophecies of judgement given to nations under the Old Covenant that have nothing to do with the Church whatsoever. Violating the basic rules of basic Biblical hermeneutics, they have pulled things out of context and developed erroneous doctrines about the

Church and have created schism, unrest, and lovelessness in the hearts of adherents to their message.

We are in at the present moment a state of crisis in the Church. It is a season of change. Times of transition are never easy. They are always difficult. In transition, there is always a need to be adaptable and pliable and sensitive to the leading of the Spirit of God. Prophecy buffs have been proclaiming fulfillment of prophecies just "on the horizon" for years. So accurate have they been that they have conveniently altered their "end-time thinking" with every fresh headline from the national press and the electronic news media. Never has the Church ever been carefully and plainly taught how to properly search the Scripture, comparing Scripture with Scripture and letting the Spirit make plain what some have made so vague. Fanning the flames of emotionalism, men have gained the ears of great multitudes who are more subject to intense emotion than the anointing that abides within.

Historically, the Church has had times when truths which were once held to and believed were forsaken because of the pressures of the days in which she was called to be a living witness of the truth. Many times the Church has been tempted and at times squeezed into the world's mold of thinking. When God would begin to bring back to the Church truths that had been long forgotten, many of God's dear people had become so used to the darkness, that the light seemed to be a lie. The end result was persecution within the Church of every fresh emphasis of truth, by those who refused to walk in the light of its power. There has never been a problem with the LIGHT. The problem has always been with our eyes. God's glory was as much filling the earth in the first five chapters of Isaiah as it was in chapter 6 when the angels made a declaration of that truth. The whole earth was filled with His glory. It was always there. The problem was that Isaiah had become so acclimated to the darkness of his day that his eyesight had dimmed. So overwhelmed was he by the glory and holiness of the Lord that he was momentarily blinded. Too much light, too soon can blind us. When the subnormal becomes normal, our faith and our expectation level to see the glory of God becomes less than God's intention for us. As a result, we ultimately judge God on the basis of our circumstances, violating the truth that as high as the heavens are above the earth so high are His thoughts above our thoughts and His ways above our ways (Isa. 55:8-9). We lose sight of His ways and His thoughts when we reduce Him to the limitations of our own willingness to believe in His Word.

The thought that there is a "hell to shun and a heaven to win" is so limited in scope that it robs us if we adhere to it as the full intention and purpose that God has for our lives. Heaven is not our destiny. God is our destiny. Eternal life is not a place, it is a Person. Knowing Him is eternal life. Heaven just happens to be where He dwells.

Jesus made it clear, however, that God wants more to bring heaven to us that to bring us to heaven. That thought was not unlike the thoughts of God under the Old Covenant. In Exodus 25, God tells Moses to construct a sanctuary so that He might "dwell among them" (25:8).

For too long we have been inundated with a mentality of "I'll fly away", and mansions on hilltops, that we have ignored the heart of God and the very clear declaration of Scripture.

If there is any repenting to be done, we need to repent for misrepresenting the God Who created the heavens and the earth for His glory and good pleasure. We need to re-turn to the revealed Will of God in the Word and discover once again the truths that we have neglected because our systems of theology did not leave room for them.

God yet has a purpose for mankind and for this planet, and until that purpose is brought to completion, the Church is not going anywhere; at least we aren't going to heaven. When Jesus said "Occupy until I come" (Luke 19:13), He wasn't merely saying "take up space and pray for the rapture". The Word *occupy* is a military term which implies a sense of administration and stewardship. In other words, He is echoing the covenant made with Adam in the garden to "be fruitful and multiply", and ultimately to fill the earth and rule over the works of God's hands.

The Spirit of God is brooding over the Church in this hour desirous to impregnate us with a fresh revelation of the fullness of God's purpose. It is imperative that we as the people of God allow Him the freedom to take us wherever He will. The Cloud of Glory is moving. It is time to move with the cloud. Movement is change. Change is never completely comfortable. Change can be unnerving and at times discouraging. But there can not be growth without change.

We must pray as did Jesus, "Thy Kingdom Come, on Earth as it is in Heaven." Not in the Millennium, but NOW in these turbulent days of history, the presence and power of the Kingdom needs to be manifest that we might accomplish what God intends for us to accomplish.

2

"WITHOUT FORM AND VOID"

Of all the appearances in the Old Testament of the Lord, there is one appearance that we take for granted and yet is perhaps of all the theophanic manifestations, the most powerful image that one could see. There are various instances of an appearance of the pre-incarnate Christ. Gideon is visited by the Angel of the Lord (Judges 7), Jacob wrestles all night with the same Angel (Genesis 32), Abraham entertains three angelic beings, the central figure being none other than the Lord Himself (Genesis 18). One can discover a number of instances of what theologians called a *theophany*. A *theophany* is basically an appearance in some tangible form of the invisible God. The greatest *theophany* however in the Old Testament was something which we so often fail to recognize. The Shekinah Cloud of

God's glory was an appearance of God in a tangible form. The Glory Cloud has such tremendous significance throughout the Scripture from Genesis through Revelation. From the very beginning the Cloud of Glory appears. When it dawned on me that Genesis 1:1-2 is a description of the brooding Glory Cloud over the chaos of the earth a series of careful and beautiful concepts began to emerge. Time and again in Scripture reference is made to the Glory Cloud and the Presence of the Spirit of the Lord. The Spirit of Glory is never divorced from the activity of God on the earth. That Glory Cloud appears time and again to repeat the pattern found in the first chapter of Genesis. What is that pattern? Very simply it is a pattern of Divine initiative moving over a chaotic situation to bring order and pattern and ultimately to prepare a place for God to come down and abide.

Moses records these opening lines for us in Genesis 1:

> In the beginning, God created the heavens and the earth. And the earth was **formless and void,** and darkness was over the surface of the deep; and the Spirit of God was **moving** over the surface of the waters.

Moses makes an interesting choice of words to describe the activity of the Spirit over the mass of the earth. As a matter of fact, when Moses describes the earth as being without form and void, he chooses a phrase which He uses only twice in all of the Pentateuch. The Hebrew word for **formless and void**, is a word which means "a desolate waste, wilderness." The Hebrew word **tohu** is the word used. The only other place this word appears in the five books of Moses is in Deuteronomy 32:10-11. That passage reads as follows:

> He found him in a desert land, and in the **howling waste** of the wilderness; He encircled him, He cared for him, He guarded him as the pupil of His eye.

Interesting enough in the verse that follows Moses uses another word which appears in Genesis 1:2. Moses describes the activity of the Spirit's Glory Cloud as **moving,** or better still, **hovering** over the surface of the waters. That verb in the Hebrew is **merahepet.** The word describes the activity of hovering over something as an eagle would hover or brood over it's young to protect and guide them to full age. Deuteronomy 32:11 is the only other place Moses ever uses the word:

> Like an eagle that stirs up its nest, that **hovers** over its young, He spread His wings and caught them, He carried them on His pinions.

The picture conveyed is very clear: As the eagle broods over her young to guide them protectively to maturity and full stature, so the Spirit of God, the Cloud of Glory brooded and hovered over the chaos at the beginning to bring to fullness and maturity that which at first was without form and void. Formlessness results in emptiness. In the original act of creation, God by His Spirit brooded over chaotic conditions to establish a pattern or a form or structure which He might ultimately fill with His Presence. Without a form or pattern, a glass could not hold water. There is an essential structure that must exist in order for there to be fullness instead of void. To be void implies first and foremost to lack structure that can contain anything. Glass that is unformed cannot contain liquid. The form makes it possible for there to be a liquid housed within it. In the original creation God first moved to create a structure at which point He intended to come down and inhabit that structure and fill it to fullness. The Spirit hovered to bring the earth from CHAOS to holy CONVOCATION. God was moving towards Sabbath Rest!

We have heard enough teaching on the Sabbath Rest that we are convinced that we understand it. Moses tells us

"And by the seventh day God completed His work which He had done; and He rested from all His work which He had done. Then God blessed the seventh day and sanctified it, because in it He rested from all His work which God had created and made" (Genesis 2:2-3).

In considering the entire concept of the Rest of God, there is something far greater than merely respite from a hard week's worth of work. Consider this thought: The Rest of God is that state of existence where things are so structured on earth so as to perfectly reflect the structure of things in heaven, that God Himself can be equally at rest here as He is in heaven. When caring people consider the purchase of a home, they generally make all sorts of adjustments to their new purchase before they move into it. They more than likely will paint it to their liking, and perhaps do some remodeling, change the carpeting, put up some wallpaper and the like. The reason being is that they have an image of what "home-sweet-home" is supposed to be. They want that new home to be a reflection of that inner image they have of who they themselves really are. Until that structure is patterned after the image they hold, they cannot be at rest in it. Therefore they work to enter in to rest. When God saw all that He made and declared it to be good, the only standard He had was the image He held of what for Him was good. God as a wise master builder knew architecturally what He was after. In looking at something without form and void He was able to start from nothing and create everything according to the pattern He held to be good. The Spirit brooded over the formlessness to bring form and pattern, to bring structure. The process began with light and ended with man. At which point God had completed His work, and it was good. Being totally satisfied, He was able to enter into His Rest, being free now to fill that structure He created and fill it to its fullness being as at home in it as He was in heaven.

The creation moved from chaos, being without form and void, to holy convocation or Sabbath Rest, the fullness of Him Who fills all in all.

But man did not appreciate the Rest of God, otherwise he would not have chosen to establish his own rest. Adam was created on the sixth day. Adam's first day of existence was God's last day of labor. Therefore his first full day of life would begin on God's day of rest. Adam was to begin to live by the Rest of God. Adam was to live his first full day of life in the fullness of God's presence. All that Adam did was to flow out of a conscious awareness of God's abiding Presence in the Cloud of Glory. When Adam chose to transgress the Rest of God, he lost his capability of enjoying God. There was no longer a place found for Adam in the garden and he was driven out from it to labor by the sweat of his brow.

In the days of the counter-cultural revolution of the late sixties and early seventies, Crosby, Stills, Nash and Young wrote a song entitled "We've got to get ourselves back to the Garden." Being a part of that entire era, I can remember the sentiments of those days and the longing for utopia in the hearts of young men and women all across America. As nice as the idea was, it is impossible for man, having chosen to find his own rest apart from the Rest of God, to work himself back into a place of admittance into a garden where all things are governed by the Rest of God.

The sad fact is that we can't get ourselves back to the Garden. We are doomed to live by our own devices when we work to find our own rest. The glory of the gospel, however, is that God brought the garden to us. In Isaiah 61 the prophet speaks:

> The Spirit of the Lord God is upon Me, because the Lord has anointed Me, to bring good news to the afflicted; He has SENT Me to bind up the broken-hearted...

The word *sent* here means to be dispatched from one place
and released to another. Christ is the embodiment of the
Glory Cloud of Genesis chapter 1. What is the Cloud of Glory
in the first three verses of Genesis is the very Son of God in
Hebrews chapter 1:

> God after He spoke long ago to the fathers in the
> prophets in many portions and in many ways, in these
> last days, has spoken to us in His Son, Whom He
> appointed heir of all things, through whom also He
> MADE THE WORLD. And He is the RADIANCE OF
> HIS GLORY AND THE EXACT REPRESENTATION
> OF HIS NATURE, AND UPHOLDS ALL THINGS BY
> THE WORD OF HIS POWER.

This One Who in the Cloud of Glory brought forth the
creation to be a reflection of the Image of God, and brought
forth man to be the full reflection of His image, is the Very
Image of God, through Whom the Father created all things.
In Him, God has chosen to seek and to save that which was
lost. He is the embodiment of the Glory of God. He is God's
Will. He is the Tree of Life, forbidden to be eaten by self-
made man, in his fallen state, except he repents of his own
works and returns to rest in God's finished work.

While we could not get ourselves back to the garden, God
brought the essence of the garden in all its fullness to us in
Jesus the Christ, anointed and sent from the Glory of God's
Presence to bring us back in touch with our original destiny:
the glory of God and the Rest of God.

We shall consider in detail how all that is included in the
Cloud of Glory is found fully in the Person of the Lord Jesus
Christ. The full implications of which for the Church will
bring us into far more than most of us dared dream was ever
possible for us in this life here and now. The problem,
however, is that when our experience does not agree with

what the Scriptural norm seems to be, we make a theology out of our excuses and consign the unfulfilled Scripture to some future age. The sad thing is, we have put off quite a number of things to the future age because we have not wanted to admit that our revelation of what the Word actually declares to be true is insufficient. Once again the problem is not the light, the problem is the darkness in our eyes.

It isn't that we don't need theology. We need theology. But if theology is impractical it is useless in the arena of life. We cannot fight life's battles with theology that is impractical. Paul takes great pains in his epistles to bring the loftiest revelations of the faith down to practical levels. A knowledge of history and doctrine is important and it has its place, but for all the teaching we have received in recent years in the flow of God the visitation of God, it seems that the more we have accumulated of the latest revelation, the colder we become to the real needs around us. The vital issue at stake in this present hour in the Church is not how much we know about the history of the faith. Neither is the issue how well we can verbalize the great doctrines of our faith, and all the current teachings that have our ears. The issue which is pressing upon us in greater ways than ever before is experiential knowledge of God. This in actuality is the arena of truth. It is the place where the rubber meets the road. In John 1:14 we are told that "the Word was made flesh and dwelt among us, and we beheld His glory". This is the crisis we are called to live in and live out in these days. God wants to flesh out the Word, Christ Himself, in us, so that all who see us behold the glory of Christ in all His fullness! The historical Jesus will not impact the Church or the harvest! The doctrinal Jesus will not impact the Church or the harvest! The only thing that will have an impact is the Word made flesh and tabernacling amongst us! It is the incarnation of the Christ in the Church that impacts life and all it involves. The Church must give birth to a fresh revelation of the Incarnate Christ in her midst. Bible School does not birth Incarnate revelation in us. Historical study does not have the capability of impregnating us with revelation that gives birth to Incarnation. The only way the Word is fleshed out in us is through the crucible of experience with God. Enoch WALKED with God. The revelation of Christ within us is what can withstand the onslaught of darkness and make us more than conquerors.

As we consider the external dimensions of the Cloud of Glory and its significance in the economy of God, it will serve no purpose unless we bring to bear the inner dimension of its significance for the Church as she is now. The Cloud of Glory is moving, and brooding. As it moves it carries out the Eternal Decrees of the Throne. To that end it came down from heaven to earth. In these days the Cloud is brooding both in and over the Church to bring the fullness of heaven down to earth, not in man-made externals or outer structures, but through the Body of Christ, created to be the fullness of Him Who fills all in all.

God wants to bring heaven in all its fullness to us more than bring us to heaven. For this cause we were born of Him. The knowledge of the GLORY of the Lord is to cover the earth as the waters cover the sea. This is not intellectual knowledge that Habakuk is speaking of, but experiential knowledge of God's glory. This can only happen as we follow the Glory Cloud of His Presence. He alone knows the WAY to His GLORY and He is the WAY.

He is brooding in us and over us to first structure us according to His Image. Once that structure finds itself in agreement with the Image of God, He then fills it with His Presence. We then become not a place for the visitation of God, but we become the very HABITATION of God.

3

THE GOVERNMENT OF GOD IS IN THE CLOUD

Then God SAID, "let there be light"; and there was light. (Genesis 1:3)

By the WORD of the Lord, the heavens were made and by the BREATH of His mouth all their host. (Psalm 33:6)

He sends forth His command to the earth, His WORD runs very swiftly. (Psalm 147:15)

Thy WORD is a lamp unto my feet, and a light unto my path. (Psalm 119:105)

As we go back and consider the prayer of Jesus in Matthew 6:9-10 where He taught His disciples to pray for the Kingdom to come on earth as it is in heaven, and we consider the implications of the picture of the Glory Cloud over the original creation, some things become very clear.

The Kingdom of God is the place where God reigns, the place where He rules, and also the realm of His rulership. Inherent in the Cloud of Glory were all three: the reign, the realm and the rule of God. Wherever God is manifest in fullness there will also be revelation of His government. In Ezekiel 1 a scenario unfolds before the eyes of this young prophet and he is overwhelmed by what he sees. There is so much that could be said about this glorious revelation he saw, but suffice it to say it was one of the many appearances of the Cloud of Glory under the Old Covenant.

Ezekiel saw wheels and living beings and fire, and a great canopy or expanse over the entire mobile Cloud, but in the midst of the Cloud he saw a THRONE. He also saw the appearance of the One Who was upon the throne. Ezekiel caught a glimpse of what was in the Cloud of Glory. Contained within the Cloud was the very throne of God.

While I firmly believe that there indeed is a literal throne upon which the Lord is seated in the heavens, the picture of the throne in the Cloud has a great deal to say about Kingdom rule and Kingdom authority. Whenever the Cloud of Glory came down the throne came down with it. Wherever the throne of God is manifest, all that would resist that throne is subdued. The sovereignty of God is a sovereignty not of mere theology but a sovereignty of power and great glory. In one place in the Psalms it says that "He spoke and it was done, He commanded and it stood fast!"(Psalm 33:9).

When the Cloud hovered over the chaotic mass of earth in the beginning, the throne of God was present. Where the throne is, there is the government of God. Where the government of God is, there you will find the decrees of God.

So it was in the beginning, God said, "let there be..." and there was. The government of God is manifest through the Word of the Lord. God creates by His Word. He reigns by His

Word. All things that God accomplished in the beginning He accomplished through the mediation of His Word.

So powerful is that Word of God that He merely speaks and His Will is done. In the Scriptures considered at the beginning of this chapter all the references about the Word of the Lord deal with a very particular term in the Hebrew. The word is **DABAR**. It occurs well over 300 times in the Old Testament. **DABAR** is a very interesting term. The **dabar** is the creative word of the Lord. It implies "to get behind and drive forward". It indicates both a word and a process. The **dabar** proceeds the event and then actually initiates and carries out the event. Isaiah describes the power of this process in Isaiah 55:10-11:

> For as the rain and the snow come down from heaven, and do not return there without watering the earth, and making it bear and sprout, and furnishing seed to the sower and bread to the eater, so shall My WORD BE WHICH GOES FORTH FROM MY MOUTH; IT SHALL NOT RETURN TO ME EMPTY, WITHOUT ACCOMPLISHING WHAT I DESIRE, AND WITHOUT SUCCEEDING IN THE MATTER FOR WHICH I SENT IT OUT.

The speaking of the **dabar** was the initial act, and the accomplishment was the final result. This idea of process is what is implied in Deuteronomy 8:3 when speaking of the gracious dealings of God:

> And He humbled you and let you be hungry, and fed you with manna which you did not know nor did your fathers know, that He might make you understand that man does not live by bread alone, but man lives by everything that PROCEEDS OUT OF THE MOUTH OF GOD.

This is the very same Scripture that Jesus quotes in the wilderness of temptation (Matthew 4:4), when the devil tries to coerce Him to abuse His power.

The **dabar** of the Lord is the PROCEEDING WORD of God. Inherent in the proceeding word of God is the power to bring into existence that which He has declared. With ease He issues a decree from the throne in the Cloud and says "Let there BE..." and there is! The Kingdom does not consist in mere words but in the demonstration of the Spirit and power. God's words are not mere words but His very BREATH is in them. His Spirit is involved in the act and process of fulfillment. The words Jesus spoke were spirit and life (John 6:23). The mind of God and the Word of God are one. In actual fact Jesus is the very LOGOS of God.

Therefore where the Cloud of Glory broods, there also is the government of God revealed, and the Will of God carried out by the creative word of the Lord.

The Church needs to be open in heart and mind to hear and obey the proceeding word of the Lord. Without the proceeding word of God we disintegrate and fragment. When Adam was created as an heir of God, he was called to a place of apprenticeship in the garden. There he was to cultivate and guard the garden, and be governed by the WORD of the Lord. The Kingdom mandate given Adam was to be fruitful, multiply, fill the earth, subdue the earth, and rule. Apart from learning to be governed by the Word of the Lord that would have been impossible.

Eden was to be the environment of Adam's apprenticeship. Here Adam was to learn to cultivate and guard what God entrusted to him. (Genesis 2:15). In actual fact Adam, under God, was to be a King-Priest in Eden. He was to cultivate the garden, a word not only implying work in the Hebrew but also worship. All we do is to be done in a consciousness of worship. Adam was also to keep the garden. A word used to describe protecting and preserving, which was used in numerous places in Leviticus to de-scribe the service of the sons of Aaron before the Lord (see Lev. 22:9). As a King-Priest under God, Adam was to be God ruled and thus so develop and grow that ultimately the borders of the garden would extend throughout the earth until the whole earth became a resting place for the glory of God.

Here in the garden by a series of choices, by the process of decision making, Adam was to learn to rule with God. God did not create Adam an automaton that blindly did what God said. Adam was a man not a robot. He was a SON not a slave. As a son he would learn to choose to be governed by the Word of the Lord and thus be transformed from innocence to the fullness of God's glory.

Unfortunately, we all know the end of the story. Adam goofed! But how well do we really understand the story? Understanding what the government of God is all about in the Book of Beginnings will help us to understand the government of God in our lives in Christ.

"Then the Lord God took the man and put him in the garden of Eden to cultivate it and keep it. And the Lord God COMMANDED the man, saying, "from any tree of the garden you may eat freely; but from the tree of the knowledge of good and evil you shall not eat, for in the day that you eat from it you shall surely die. Then the Lord God said it is not good for man to be alone; I will make him a helper suitable for him" (Genesis 2:15-18).

The first thing we ought to recognize about Adam's apprenticeship is that the Lord gave Adam some specific responsibilities and gave him a specific command. Adam's first sphere of responsibility was in the area of cultivation. He was to cultivate and develop the garden. Cultivation leads to enlargement and expansion. Yet Adam was also to keep or guard the garden. As a good steward he was to guard all that was entrusted to him, and preserve it for God even as it grew. The question must arise at this point in our minds: from what must Adam protect the garden? Or perhaps from *whom* must Adam protect the garden? It is a valid question in light of the command given him. The next observation to be made is that in the garden there already is abundant provision for all his needs. Before he even knew what hunger was, God had already provided food for the eating. All this was for Adam's enjoyment. Yet there was one tree which Adam was forbidden to eat from.

In the middle of the garden there was a tree that God called the tree of the KNOWLEDGE OF GOOD AND EVIL. Some have mistakenly called this the tree of good and evil. It is not referred to as such, but rather as the tree of the KNOWLEDGE of good and evil. The word used here for knowledge implies experiential knowledge. It is a tree that when one eats of it immediately there is an experiential understanding of duality. Good and evil existing together in the mind and heart of man is the cause of great sorrow, unrest and upheaval. It is a tree of humanistic evaluation. It is a tree of independence from the government of God. Why be ruled by a WORD outside yourself when you can have the full experience and decide for yourself what is good and what is evil?

Adam was by no means ignorant. He had a great mind and a creative spirit because he was made in God's image. He very much was *like God*. If you are made in the image of God you are very much *like God*. It does not take much expertise to discover that truth when logically thought out and considered.

So Adam had some very clear directives from the Lord. He was to cultivate (a priestly function of worship and work) and to keep (a jealous guarding for God and protecting for God what was rightfully His), and he was to freely enjoy all things that God had blessed him with. The only thing he could not do was eat of the tree of the knowledge of good and evil, for death would inevitably result. Without a doubt if a tree of the knowledge of good and evil existed, so must have good and evil existed in the universe. So too, Adam was told that death also existed. Though he had never experienced death, by the implication of the command from God it was obviously not something to hope for. Adam therefore knew it was destructive.

All of these facts were made known to Adam by direct revelation from God. All of this occurred before Eve was created. In the account in Scripture, what follows is that God desires to create a mate for Adam. Yet He brings Adam through the process of naming all the animals that God had created. Imagine the *creativity* that existed in the mind of Adam to name all the animals. Yet in the entire process of naming all the animals, Adam was looking to see if any of the creatures resembled him and none bore his likeness. God, all the while, wanted to bring Adam to the conclusion that thus far there was nothing suitable created to share the reign of the earth with him. At that point the Lord causes a deep sleep to fall upon Adam and fashions a help-meet out of his side to rule alongside him.

Genesis 3 opens with the introduction of a new character. The character is a talking serpent. We have no idea how long after Eve was created that the serpent appears, but there was a certain amount of time that had obviously elapsed. His character is less than noble. He immediately seeks to slander God by challenging the Word of God. "Indeed" he says, (can't you just hear the tone of his voice?) "Has God said, 'you shall not eat from any tree of the garden'?" Eve answers this talking snake by letting him know he is somewhat misinformed. It isn't 'any tree' they can't eat from but the 'tree in the midst of the garden'. The observation at this point must be made for the sake of the evidence of Scripture. The serpent came to Eve not to Adam. We are told that the command not to eat of the forbidden tree came to Adam before Eve was created. Therefore, did Eve hear the command from God or from Adam? She was given the information from her husband. In II Timothy 2:14 Paul tells us plainly "And it was not Adam who was deceived, but the woman being QUITE DECEIVED fell into transgression."

If someone has had a face to face encounter and dialogue with someone else and has heard word for word what is true and what is false, it doesn't matter who comes along later to try to slander the character of the person who told you, or infer that the person did not say that thing at all, because you cannot be deceived, you had the experience. You can only be deceived if you did not get the information first hand. This has far reaching implications. The first temptation that came to Eve was to doubt the ability of her husband to hear clearly from God. The serpent was implying that Adam was wrong. This is all being done very subtly, by inference. These are not direct accusations, but they are inferred. There is an immediate attempt to break down the trust between the man and his wife. If the serpent can divide them he can cause them to fail to rule in harmony over the creation of God. Jesus Himself said that a house divided against itself cannot stand.

Unfortunately the fact that Eve entered into conversation with the serpent put her in a position of weakness. There is a further question that arises at this point. Adam was commanded to guard or protect the garden. Somehow this intruder managed to wander into the garden unnoticed. Where was Adam? When the woman begins to explain that the only tree they could not eat from was the tree of the knowledge of good and evil, lest they die, the serpent begins to literally call God a liar. This a direct accusation. He says "you shall not die" and then implies that God is afraid of losing control over them for they would become like God. This too is inference. Please consider this fact: being made in the image of God according to Genesis 1:26 implies that

Adam was already like God. He did not need to become what he already was.

The serpent is inferring that they are not something that God declares already to be true about them. By that point she was in too deep where she could not swim, and she was sucked in. She saw that the tree was good for food, and that it was a delight to the eyes, and that the tree was desirable to make one wise and so she took of the fruit and she ate (Genesis 3:6).

Many of us have struggled with why God even gave man the option of a tree like this one. If the tree was not there, Eve never would have been in difficulty. There is a need for us to realize that God is not afraid of the free will of man. He did not create robots. He created us with the power to make decisions. The freedom to fail was built into the process of taking dominion. There was a wisdom beyond anything we can ever comprehend in the placing of that tree in the garden. We have for too long seen that choice as a negative aspect of our being. It was actually a tremendous positive aspect of our being. God so esteemed the man and woman He made in His image that He gave them the freedom to choose for themselves, and learn to make decisions on the basis of knowledge gained, and thus learn to grow in the knowledge of God. The question then arises, how could they know good and evil and whether it was a wise choice except they experience it for themselves? Answering that question may not be as difficult as one might think. The Word of the Lord is not void of the Spirit of the Lord. God's Word is not divorced form His very Person and character. Jesus said the letter kills, but the Spirit gives life. Adam had an encounter not merely with a WORD from God, the Word came with a revelation of the gracious and loving Person Who gave it. The Word issued forth from Imminent Goodness Himself. He is not only Imminent Goodness, He is Imminent Love, Mercy, Grace, and Peace all mingled into One.

When Adam encountered God, he encountered the Perfection of Love. Adam did not know sin at this point, so there
was no fear in his life. All he knew was a childlike trust and
love for His Father God. A suspicious thought did not even
enter his mind, doubt was non-existent. He lived in perfect
trust and confidence with the Lord God, who was his
Father.

When the serpent showed up he could not tempt Adam,
for Adam had tasted of the goodness of the Lord. The
serpent could, however, tempt Eve. As the Word of God is
not divorced from the nature and character of His Person, so
the words of the serpent are not divorced from his nature
and character either. Whether Eve never experienced good
or evil herself should not have been the issue, because just
by the tone of the serpent's voice and the nature of his
method of questioning, enough bells should have gone off to
indicate that danger was near.

But it all seemed to happen faster than she could think.
That was exactly her problem. She disregarded what she
intuitively knew and tried to rely on her own rational
ability to reason the argument out in her mind. That, in
essence, is the nature of temptation. Temptation does not
become sin until we close ourselves off to the intuitive voice
of a Spirit-controlled conscience and try to use our own
limited thinking to overcome a power greater than ourselves. Once the enemy has us there, he has us by deception.
The end result is indeed, death.

Now that we have established that Eve was indeed
deceived, the next question arises. Where was Adam when
all this was going on? Why didn't he come to the rescue? The
Scripture does not leave any room for wondering in this
regard either. "...she took from its fruit and ate, and she gave
also to her husband, **WITH HER**, and he ate" (Genesis 3:6).

The entire episode of Eve being deceived was all under
the watchful eye of the vigilant, "garden-guarding" Adam.

Can you imagine? It says he was WITH HER. He allowed the serpent to deceive her, and did not try to stop her from doing what was going to knowingly result in death. Adam knew full well the implications of such an act and allowed it to take place anyway. To whom is the greater judgement to come? To Adam of course, because while Eve was deceived, Adam was WILFULLY DISOBEDIENT. Adam had opposed the government of God by his disobedience. The result was indeed death. They lost their childlike innocence that enabled them to trust implicitly the Word of the Lord without question. Separation from God's conscious Presence followed immediately thereafter.

In the one choice Adam made, so much was lost! What great sorrow must have been experienced both in heaven and in Adam's heart at that moment. When it dawned upon Him what his choice meant, it was too late. He had already fallen.

It is no wonder Jesus came to seek and save THAT WHICH was lost, not just those who lost it. When we consider revival and restoration and the forward momentum of the Church, we tend to think we are moving on and moving forward. In actuality, from God's perspective, we are moving backwards to His original intent for us. He is restoring to us THAT WHICH WE ONCE HAD BUT LOST. All the miracles and acts of power Jesus did, He did as a Man under the government of God. He did them as the Last Adam. When we see Jesus walking on the water, He was simply being ruled by the Word of the Lord and not by the elements. That is the very power Adam had before the fall. That is dominion. Jesus performed all His miracles and acts of power in cooperation with the Spirit to fulfill the Old Covenant. What is amazing to me is that He said we in the New Covenant would do greater works.

I can't imagine anything greater than walking on water or raising the dead. I know that theologians have their neat little explanations for what Jesus REALLY MEANT when He said we would do greater works. Deep inside, however, their theological explanation is really a cover for the spirit of unbelief that lies deep in their hearts, for the same sinister force that deceived the woman into doubting the veracity of the proceeding word of the Lord, has convinced us of the same. Henceforth our theology leaves no room for the limitless creativity of a limitless Creator, Who possesses the power to cause us to yet do greater works. Quite honestly I would just settle for the lesser works of walking on water and raising the dead. It at least is a good place to start.

God help us to become men and women who allow the government of God be established in us by the Word of the Lord as He speaks out of the Cloud of Glory in our lives.

The great curse of the Church is that we still tend to eat at the tree of the knowledge of good and evil. We live in the limitation of rationalism for we feel safer to be ruled by our minds and our own ability to solve our problems, than by the LIVING and ABIDING Word of God. The reason is simple: If God indeed does still speak by His Spirit, and we hear Him speak, we would have to OBEY what He decrees. The consequences of even admitting we might be mistaken would so shake up our systems of theology that we would rather not hear from God. The Cloud is hovering to restore to us the cognitive reality of the WORD of the Lord. Let us pray that as God restores the ability to hear that proceeding word that He would restore our ability to be mature enough to do whatever He tells us to do.

So be it!

4

THE SOUND OF HIS PRESENCE

"And they heard the sound of the Lord God walking in the garden in the cool of the day, and the man and his wife hid themselves from the presence of the Lord God among the trees of the garden." (Genesis 3:8)

The Authorized Version reads "...they heard the VOICE.." The New American Standard more accurately describes the event with the word SOUND. The word in Hebrew which Moses uses here is "qol". Most scholars agree that the word **qol** is not a word used to describe speaking conversationally. It actually depicts the sound of approaching judgement. When we speak of the coming of the Lord in judgement, one thing which we must realize is that there are many times when the Lord has come in history to judge. This appearing of the Lord in Genesis 3 is the first time that the Lord comes in judgement. The word **qol** is used elsewhere in Scripture to describe the sound of God's presence approaching. Psalm 18:13 is one such instance: "The Lord also THUNDERED in the heavens and the Most High UTTERED His VOICE." In the third chapter of the prophecy of Joel, the prophet speaks not only of the restoration of the Church, but the judgement of the nations through the Church, and in verse 16 he records these words for us: "And the Lord ROARS from Zion, and utters His VOICE from Jerusalem, and the heavens and the earth TREMBLE."

These passages which use the word **qol** far from describe a pleasant sound. They describe the fearful sound of the Lord approaching in judgement. Usually when we read Genesis 3:8 we read it as though the Lord was taking His evening constitutional in the garden totally unaware of what was happening and when the quiet whisper of His gentle voice was heard, Adam and Eve ran and hid. Unfortunately this is so far from the truth that it diminishes the weight of the passage. This was the approaching sound of the Lord in judgement and Adam and Eve were terrified at the SOUND of His Presence. It is no wonder they ran to hide. Doesn't the writer to the Hebrews tell us it is a "terrifying thing to fall into the hands of the Living God?" (Hebrews 10:31).

The moment Adam fell there was an awareness that judgement was inevitable. It was the same terrifying sound (**qol**) the sons of Israel heard at the foot of Mount Sinai when the mountain was covered in thick darkness and gloom, and the trumpet was blown, and the mountain burned with fire while the Lord spoke from the midst of the fire and the nation trembled at His appearing (Deuteronomy 4:11-12).

In his book, *Images of the Spirit,* author Meredith Kline does an excellent study regarding this text and uncovers some clues as to what the actual phraseology of the sound of the Lord and the "cool of the day" actually refer to. For those theologically minded, his text is excellent reading and study material. The phrase "in the cool of the day" is rather misleading as translated. It has therefore caused much controversy over its actual meaning. It is only used here in Genesis 3:8 and nowhere else in the Scripture. The New American Standard, makes the footnote that the word for "cool" is literally WIND or BREEZE. It is the same word used for SPIRIT. The Spirit is often in Scripture linked with the sound of God's Presence. The Spirit of the day at the approach of His coming was a spirit of judgement.

When we are free from guilt, and free from sin, there is no fury in the Sound of His approach. However, when guilt is present, so too is fear present. Guilt and fear are the result of the choice one makes to act independently of the wisdom of God.

Adam and Eve were full of fear. Their fear drove them from His presence in an effort to hide. It is actually foolish to even think you can hide from Him Who is all-transcendent and ever-present. All things are naked and bare before Him. David cries out "Where can I go from your Spirit? Or where can I flee from Your Presence?" (Psalm 139:7). The truth is that you cannot hide from God or try to run away from Him. Yet inevitably many of us, do just that. We tend to think that only those outside of Christ are hiding from God, but tragically many of God's own children, by covenant birthright in Christ try to hide from Him out of guilt and fear. Did the Sound of His Presence change from Genesis 2 to Genesis 3? Not at all. What did change was Adam's perception of God. Guilt and fear changed the way his senses responded to the Sound of His coming. God gave man his five senses so that they might serve him in his service to the Lord. There is nothing wrong with our sense of knowledge. It is God-given and not carnal. The problem however is when in our inner man we have transgressed the covenant, guilt and fear begin to flow across the fiber of our spirit into every part of our being to the outermost part of our existence. Our nervous system responds to the stimuli of His Presence on the basis of internal distortion rather than internal harmony.

Man was not built to be able to handle sin. Sin is not natural. Sin is a twisting of the image of God in man. Sin has marred the faculty of man, and caused him to see all things in light of his experiential knowledge of good and evil. That knowledge is limited and cursed. It is like a filter on a camera lens that is purposely used to distort a picture that the camera is taking. The filter distorts the reality of what is. If reality is distorted in our spirit, it will also be distorted in our mind, our mouth and our ears.

When Adam fell he lost the ability to perceive clearly. He forfeited the truth for a lie. He forfeited the truth that he already was in God's likeness and image, in order to become like God. How tragic.

In verse 9 we read: "Then the Lord called to the man, and said to him, "Where are you?" As we consider this question we have to ask another question. Didn't God know where Adam was? If He did not know, then He is not God, for God is Omniscient, knowing all things. For whose benefit then was God asking the question? For Adam's benefit of course. In asking the question of Adam, God wanted Adam to admit the truth as to where he was. In God asking where Adam was He was asking not for his physical location as much as his present STATE of existence. "Adam, where are you internally at the moment? What state are you in?" Psalm 51:6 David declares "Behold, Thou dost desire **truth** in the innermost being.." Jesus said true worship can only be true worship if it is in spirit and **truth** (John 4:24). Adam had been given a sphere to cultivate. He was to cultivate and guard the garden. This was his sphere of worship. Worship is more than what you do, it is who you are. The coming of the Lord in the garden was to be a time when Adam could admit in honesty as to where He was.

Adam hid at the sound of the Lord's coming, and thus signified that he refused to admit where he was. Actions are always consistent, even when veiled, with where we really are. Adam really did not want to face God, because to face God meant he would have to face himself, his own actions and take responsibility for those actions.

When Adam ran as far as he could, and God called, he realized that he had to give an answer. His answer was that he heard the sound, and hid out of fear because he was naked (3:10).

Naked? What does it mean to be naked? Surely Adam was no different in appearance now than the day he was created. God knew exactly how he created man and intended for him to live. This was a new revelation. And it had a negative connotation. Adam inferred that it was evil by his confession. But God asks another question: "Who told you you were naked?" In actuality no one told Adam. It was an awareness that came as the result of an experience. That experience was something he was warned not to involve himself with before it ever happened. God then asks the next logical question in light of the piece of information Adam gave Him. "Have you eaten from the tree of which I commanded you not to eat?" This, too, was a rhetorical question. God knew what Adam had done. His desire was for Adam to take responsibility for what he had done.

When the question was put to Adam, the Scripture reveals how irresponsible Adam chose to be. His response was "The woman whom Thou gavest to be with me, she gave me from the tree and I ate." Basically Adam was not just blaming Eve, he blamed God. This was an attempt on Adam's part to avoid the unpleasant possibility of God's judgement. He was not just lying to God, he was lying to himself. He did not want to admit he willfully chose to eat from the forbidden tree. He can't believe that he could do such a thing of his own volition, and yet he did. He would rather live in a certain level of deception than admit the truth.

Why the fear of admitting the truth? To admit the truth would mean that Adam had dishonored God, and broke covenant with God. The shame and reproach of dishonoring a loving and gracious Father was too painful. Yet that would have been the proper response. That would have been godly sorrow. That would have been true repentance. God wanted an honest answer from His son. He created all things freely for him to enjoy. It was His delight to give Adam rulership over the works of His hands.

Is it possible that had Adam admitted the truth to God instead of lying and projecting his guilt on Eve and ultimately God, that he might not have been banished from the garden? Doesn't the Scripture declare that there is forgiveness with God that He might be feared? God is slow to anger and abounding in loving kindness. He longs to be gracious. God, however, cannot be gracious if we choose to deceive ourselves and deny the truth.

God desired Adam to take responsibility for where he was. A mature son would do that and make his Father's heart glad. Yet he revealed the level of his immaturity by his dishonesty. That dishonesty was based on fear. Where did fear come from? It came from a distorted view of reality that had it's roots in the experience of dualism: good and evil. The tree of life was a tree of wholeness and singularity. It was a tree that had all things relating to a central theme: LIFE. The tree of the knowledge of good and evil is a tree that misrepresents reality. It is a tree that declares life is fragmented and at the center of reality there is constantly going to be a struggle of good and evil and the best you can hope for is to become strong enough to overcome evil. The lie is that once you enter into a struggle to overcome that duality you are already declaring that you have rejected the truth. God did not create the universe as fragments. The cosmos and the universe were created as a whole, all to be rightly related and subject to the Will and governing of the Creator. His character and personality was imparted to the whole of His creation, and it derives its meaning from its relationship to Him. Apart from Him, all things lose their significance. All things were created by Him for His pleasure. In actuality, since the creation, God has been moving towards the summing up of all things in Christ both in heaven and in the earth. (Ephesians 1:10)

Apart from God, man chooses to live in a dualistic environment, where he is forced by way of experience to learn how to combat evil with good. The tragedy being, that man's experiential concept of goodness is not at all like the goodness of God. God's commentary is that there is NONE GOOD, NO NOT ONE (Romans 3:10)!

All of man's attempts to correct the injustices of society, and the evils that exist are futile, because man, by his own choice, approaches life from a dualistic consciousness. Good and evil coexist in the world, so I must work at being good and fighting evil. Man fights himself in the process because good and evil are from the same tree. They are two sides of a coin that God condemned long ago in the garden of Eden.

To maintain that type of world view is to actually admit there is no need for God. But life by its very definition in Scripture is not found in the battle of good and evil. God is LIFE.

To live and eat from the tree of knowledge of good and evil is to live symptomatically. As long as man wants to deal with symptoms he will never be cured. When in Mark 11 Jesus cursed the fig tree, we are told that it withered from the roots up (verse 20). To deal with the fruit of the tree that God cursed is to deal with symptoms. Unregenerate man has chosen to have a world view that is dualistic. It is a world view that constantly speaks of cause and effect, but in practice avoids the reality of cause and effect for the same reason Adam avoided reality in his encounter in the garden with the Lord. Eliminating bad fruit from a tree, only paves the way for more bad fruit to grow. But man would rather live there thinking that good will ultimately triumph over evil, if he just tries hard enough. It is the greatest lie ever manufactured.

If man is God, as the humanists declare, which is the basic lie of Genesis 3:1-5, then man has the power by his own experience to totally correct all the evils in the universe and reign supreme.

History makes it rather evident that no matter how noble the aspirations of fallen man, no matter what honor is bestowed upon his discoveries by his colleagues, he has only succeeded in perpetuating the age old lie that he can achieve dominion apart from God.

When John the Baptist appears in the wilderness preaching, he makes a rather interesting comment: "The axe is laid at the ROOT of the trees..." There is only one remedy for the tree of the knowledge of good and evil. We must lay the axe of TRUTH AT THE ROOT of its growth in our lives. We must admit where we are and agree with God that ultimately we cannot break God's laws, because they are built into His creation. If we attempt to break His law, it will, in actuality, break us.

It is not God Who moved, it was Adam who changed his address. Isaiah records these words: "Therefore the Lord LONGS to be gracious to you, And therefore He WAITS ON HIGH TO HAVE COMPASSION on you. For the Lord is a God of **justice**; How blessed are all those who LONG FOR HIM!" (Isaiah 30:18). God longed to be gracious to Adam, but God first requires truth before He can give grace. "For thus says the Lord God, the Holy One of Israel, 'In repentance and rest you shall be saved, In quietness and trust is your strength.' But you were not willing." (Isaiah 30:15). Repentance precedes grace. And very simply, repentance is admitting where you are, and realizing that what you thought was true, was a lie. And once you exchange the lie for the truth, grace and compassion will flow to you from your Creator.

For too long we have dealt with *sins*. Even unregenerate man tries to deal with his *sins*. People resolve day after day to break certain habits, change their attitudes, be more loving, let go of maladaptive behavior patterns that are destructive. Some even find a degree of success, all without God. But *sins* are the fruit. *Sins* are symptomatic. The ROOT is what the Bible calls original **SIN**. The axe of the gospel is laid at the ROOT OF THE TREE. God comes to us and asks us where we are in relationship to Him, not in relationship to our sins. The root of sin is our attitude towards God. That is why Paul preached repentance towards God, not repentance towards sins. If man will deal with the root, and eliminate the root, the fruit will no longer be able to grow.

It takes great fortitude to deal with the root, for we will have to admit that we are the clay and He is the potter. We are the creature and He is the Creator. We will have to admit that we can only really KNOW truth as we are rightly related to Him who is TRUTH. Adam didn't think twice about eating of the wrong tree. He wasn't as wise as he thought he was. The root of the tree of the knowledge of good and evil is a mystery that the Bible calls the mystery of iniquity. Unregenerate man will never understand that mystery apart from God. And as long as unregenerate man, and even regenerate man chooses to follow a program of experience and self-effort to overcome evil, he will succeed in maintaining and cultivating the very spiritual life and energy of the serpent's lie.

"But solid food is for the mature, who because of practice have their senses trained to discern good and evil." (Heb. 5:14). Discerning good and evil is worlds apart from knowing

good and evil. The mature are those who have come to
honor the Word of God, as the only reliable source of
government in their lives, and by learning to listen to the
voice of God, they also recognize that voice which is not of
God, and steer clear of the trap of having to experience the
lie in order to know the truth.

When Adam rejected the Word of the Lord, he rejected
the very government of God. God governs His creation by
His Word. As expressed before, His Word and His character
are inseparable. To reject the government of God is to
accept the lie that your own evaluation and judgement is
sufficient for growth. The result is the government of satan,
of ignorance and/or oppression, the end of which is death
even as the Lord had made clear beforehand.

The visitation of God, the sound of His coming in the
Glory Cloud is to be a time of accountability for the people of
the Lord. The Sound of His coming in the Cloud of Glory
created controversy in the garden because Adam fell. The
Creator-Lord was desirous of total honesty in His son and
did not find it. Adam did not want to be brutally honest with
himself. When Adam fell, he was IN THE GARDEN. When
the Cloud of Glory ushered in the sound of the Lord's
Presence it was IN THE GARDEN. There is every reason to
believe that restoration could have taken place IN THE
GARDEN. All that the Lord required was HONESTY in
Adam. Adam chose rather to be alienated from the TRUTH.
As a result, there could only be one thing left for Adam: he
had to be banished from the garden. Remember that the
garden was the place that housed the Tree of Life and the
Presence of the Lord. The Glory Cloud and all that was
contained therein found a resting place on earth even as it
rested in heaven. Man, however, forfeited the right, by dishonesty, to remain in the FULLNESS OF HIS PRESENCE.

Isaiah tells us that the "resting place of His feet will be
glorious" (11:10). God's feet found a resting place in Eden.

There His Glory abided. But Eden was not His ultimate intention. Man was to be the ultimate resting place of the Glory of His Presence. Man was created for the GLORY of God. Adam fell, and missed the mark. The Scripture tells us that in Adam, we all fell short of the GLORY of the Lord.

The sons of God have only one true HOME. We are called to be the habitation of the Lord. Christ as the Son of Man came to seek and save that which was lost. He came to restore man to God's original intention. Christ came to bring into existence a BODY for the Presence of God's fullness. "Sacrifices and burnt offerings Thou has not desired, but A BODY THOU HAS PREPARED FOR ME" (Hebrew 10:5). This was the purpose for the coming of Christ. Father was through Him paving the way for a BODY to be brought forth to contain His fullness. For the intent of the Father is to fill the earth with the glorious presence of the Christ. Isn't it interesting that Christ, the Head, cannot be complete without His Body? Didn't He Himself say "The foxes have holes, the birds of the air have nests, but the Son of Man has nowhere to lay His head" (Matthew 8:20)?

The ultimate resting place for the Head, even Christ, is His Body, the Church. The ultimate resting place for the Body is the fullness of God dwelling within it.

The Cloud of Glory that ushered in the visitation of His presence in the garden was a crucial time for Adam. At the moment of visitation, Adam chose alienation and lost the opportunity to become God's place of habitation.

Adam chose alienation, and alienation led to disorientation. He was driven from the garden, from the Presence of the Lord and from the Tree of Life. No longer were all things freely available to enjoy. He found the ground cursed because of his choice. He found family relationships cursed, and he found himself dealing with death as a reality all around and within him, along with an acute awareness that there was no hope at least during his lifetime for change.

Death came to his spirit and inevitably it would come to his flesh as well. Emotions he never knew existed became familiar to him: hopelessness, frustration, despair, greed, envy, anger, and the like. How far he had fallen!

Adam lost his internal integrity. He lost his ability to hear God clearly. The separation was not just physical it was most keenly spiritual and internal. His inner man, which prior to his choice knew unbroken communion with God, now had lost the intuitive ability to respond to the Presence of the Lord.

While God did not lose His position of ruler of the earth, Adam forfeited his right to rule because he believed the lie of the serpent. While Adam lost his power to have dominion over creation, God did not lose His dominion over the earth. The earth is the LORD'S and the FULLNESS THEREOF. God never gave His authority to the serpent. It was Adam who aligned himself with the serpent not God. God still was KING and that has never changed. What God lost was a man to rule with Him over the works of His hands. The heart of God longed for fellowship with a son who would share the rulership of the universe with Him. By working through a man full of His glory God would fill the earth with His fullness. God was never taken by surprise at the fall. God was grieved by the fall, but He did not suffer loss.

Sometimes our theology makes our God to be anemic and dependent upon the creature. God is totally self-sufficient and needs nothing. His love causes Him to desire fellowship, and to share the fullness of His glory with a people for His possession. Yet if we follow a line of thinking that places the serpent in a position of authority over the works of His hands we have moved beyond the realm of Scriptural authority and bought a lie.

The serpent, too, was cursed by God. The serpent was not given a place of dominion, he was consigned to eat the dust of the earth. He was to be a scavenger for all his days, until the time when his ability to lie and deceive would be totally destroyed by One Who when He came, would be fully an expression of the habitation of God in the earth. He Who would come would, by His obedience, overrule the disobedience of the first Adam, and enable the Creator to entrust to a Man the rulership over the works of His hands. Until He would come, the serpent would attempt to maintain control by his lies to the disoriented man who now lost something of the original image of God's glory. And by his own dishonesty was no longer free to see the issues clearly but by his own choice, would live in willful deception to the lie.

To deny the lie would involve now a tremendous internal fortitude to go against the tide of that which was now under a curse. That fortitude is totally impossible apart from the Spirit of God.

Man's situation apart from God was and is totally hopeless. This is not due to God, but due rather to man. Even the power the serpent has he only has because man believes his lie. Man is still responsible for where he is before God. On the final day of judgement, none will be able to blame the serpent, blame God, or blame anyone else. It will be evident to all that God is just in all His judgements.

God never gave the dominion of the earth over to the serpent. When the Scripture says that the whole world (cosmos) lies in the evil one, and when he is called the prince of the power of the air, it is not referring to him in the place of dominion apart from man's willful disobedience. Man is still accountable, otherwise this statement is totally false:

> For the wrath of God is revealed from heaven against all ungodliness and unrighteousness of men, who suppress the truth in unrighteousness, because that which is KNOWN about God is EVIDENT to them. For since the creation of the world His invisible attributes, His eternal power, and divine nature, have been clearly seen, being understood through what has

seen, being understood through what has been made,
so that they are without excuse.

For even though they KNEW God, they did not
HONOR HIM AS GOD, or give thanks; but they
became futile in their speculations and their foolish
heart was darkened. (Romans 1:18-21).

It is crucial to our understanding to realize that God is the
Ruler-Supreme over the earth and all that it contains. Satan
is a pseudo-ruler. The kingdom of darkness is a pseudo-
kingdom. When a person chooses to be deceived, there is a
certain authority that the darkness has over him, and that
satan has over him. But it is rulership fabricated around a
lie, not the truth. Truth is found only in God. Freedom is
found only in truth. When the truth is allowed to penetrate
the darkness of man's soul he immediately recognizes that
Jesus IS LORD! The whole earth is His Glory!

If satan truly had authority it would have been acknowl-
edged when the Lord God pronounced His judgement at
His coming after Adam's fall. Adam's fall followed the fall of
satan. But God, dearly beloved, never fell! He cannot fall!
His Kingdom is an EVERLASTING KINGDOM and His
DOMINION ENDURES THROUGH ALL GENERATIONS!
(Psalm 145:13). David addresses these verses to his KING
long before redemption in Christ was fully realized. Time
and again in the law and the prophets and the writings of
what we know as the Old Testament, it is ascribed to God
that He sits as King over all the earth and the universe and
that His sovereignty rules over all. If HE was not King, the
He could not have authority to judge Adam, judge Eve,
judge the serpent, and declare the end from the beginning.
But He is King, and therefore at the Sound of His coming,
Adam, Eve, and the serpent were ultimately given the
absolute judgement of the One Who has the right to rule.

5

THE CLOUD OF GLORY
IS MOVING

Since the Lord, Who is King, was not taken by surprise, His ultimate purpose would be fully realized. In His grace and mercy therefore He began immediately after judgement was pronounced to act redemptively on man's behalf. Couched within the curse of the serpent, was the promise of restoration. "And I will put enmity between you and woman, and between your SEED and her SEED; He shall crush you on the head, and you shall crush Him on the heel" (Genesis 3:15).

There would ultimately come forth from the seed of the woman a *manchild* Who Himself would crush the power and authority of the venomous serpent's lie, by stepping on his head. In the process of destroying the very power center of the lie, this manchild would Himself experience His heel being crushed. The last fatal bite of the serpent would finally end his power forever, and though he would bite the heel of the manchild, that heel would once and for all end his ability to hold mankind in bondage by the lie. The tempter has no substance to offer that can back up his lie, but the lie is enough to destroy the image of God's glory in His creation.

God made provision for Adam and Eve, even though they were under the curse. He covered their nakedness through the death of a sacrifice and established a system of sacrifice, by the shedding of blood for the remission of sins.

Adam and Eve had relations and Eve gave birth to a son. In the actual Hebrew it is clear that she believed that the son she bore was the promised conqueror. "I have gotten a manchild, the Lord" (Genesis 4:1). Eve believed that this was the Messiah the Conqueror promised in Genesis 3:15. It wasn't, of course, but it was the hope of every woman of the Old Covenant nation that the first born son that opened the womb would indeed be that One Whom God promised would crush the head of the serpent.

At the heights of Eden the Glory of God abided. Man would come from time to time to the gateway of the garden and present his sacrifices before the Lord, but was never allowed in the garden to that most holy place where the Tree of Life was located.

Nevertheless, it was the desire of God to dwell on earth with His people as comfortably as He dwelt in heaven. Therefore He begins to act and move redemptively in history to 'seek and to save that which was lost'. Man was created to live in the fullness of Father's glorious Presence. Adam was to have risen to maturity in sonship, and as a co-ruler of the universe, share the responsibilities of Him in Whose Image he was created.

From time to time in redemptive history the same Spirit that hovered over creation and brooded over that which was formless, appears and broods over places and people to bring them on into a greater revelation of His redemptive purposes.

The Glory Cloud appears again and again with the same stirring and sounds as at first. Adam never could have realized the far reaching effects of his sin. All mankind would be as a result, more prone to live in deception rather than in the truth. All were included in Adam's fall, and according to Paul in Romans, God shut up all men in Adam's disobedience, in order that the revelation of His mercy would be that much greater. As Adam was alienated by his own choice from God, so all men therefore were alienated from God. But as mentioned already, alienation leads to disorientation.

The word 'orient' literally means 'eastward'. Isn't it interesting that there was a garden 'eastward' in Eden. When man fell, he became dis-ORIENTED from the GLORY CLOUD. He was banished from the center of internal integrity. What should have been totally familiar became totally unfamiliar, and that which God forbade should have remained unfamiliar to Adam, but because the realm of the familiar for him. Thus he was disoriented from reality. The only way back to proper orientation was the grace of the Creator. It would take a sovereign act of His Will and His sovereign working in the lives of individuals to bring them back to proper orientation to God.

Generations after Adam had come and gone, and the flood had swept away the entire populous of the earth, Noah's sons began to replenish the earth and ten generations later, after hundreds of years, God chose to proceed with His restoration program. In Ur of the Chaldees, where idolatry and paganism ran rampant, where mankind had reached the epitome of disorientation from God, the glory of God appeared to a man named Abram. In Genesis 12 we are told that the word of the Lord came to Abram while yet in Ur of the Chaldees. In Acts 7:2, the Holy Spirit gives us a bit more insight into the situation through the words of Stephen: "Hear me brethren, and fathers! The **GOD OF GLORY** appeared to our father Abraham...".

This little phrase, the God of glory, has tremendous significance. Man had alienated himself from the Presence of God, and had disoriented himself far from the garden of God. After the flood there no longer was a garden. God desired a place on earth for His glory to inhabit. By the time Abraham was alive we have little account in Scripture of appearances of His glory.

God, in His grace, takes initiative and reveals Himself in His glory to a star worshipper. One who was disoriented from his Creator is about to be reoriented by his Creator. But it takes something 'disorienting' to get an alienated person out of his state of what for him is reality. It took a revelation of the glory of God to undo Abram.

It was the glory of God that caused Abram to leave everything and look for a CITY that resembled the glory of the Architect Who promised that such a CITY existed. God wanted to bring His creation from disorientation to reorientation.

The Cloud of Glory was moving on in redemptive history to seek and to save that which was lost. Mankind had become secure in the lie. This was not the Will of God. In order to produce a people for God's own possession it was necessary to break the power of the lie by bringing the substance of truth to bear on the hearts and minds of men. God sought for a man whom He could take from disorientation to reorientation. Abram was that man.

As we seek to grow in maturity in our relationship to God the Father through Christ, the spiritual implications of the call of Abraham have applications for us in the New Covenant.

As we consider the call of Abram it will become clear as to the process that goes on in our lives as God brings us to a

clearer understanding of His redemptive purposes in our
lives when the glory of God impacts us and demands of us a
total change of vision, perspective and reality.

Now the Lord said to Abram, Go forth from your
COUNTRY, and from your RELATIVES, and from
your FATHER'S HOUSE, to the land which I WILL
SHOW YOU. (Genesis 12:1).

The Lord called Abram by His glory out from one place
into another. He was to leave country, family, and his
father's house. The promise being that if he left all that, God
would show him a land, bless him, bless his seed, bless all
nations, make his name great, and bless all who bless him,
and curse all who curse him.

To leave his country, Abram had to move beyond the
borders and limitations and boundaries into which he was
born. For each of us, our 'country' is different, it can very
well be our nationality or our ethnicity, but it is also more
than that. All of us were raised within a set of boundaries
that for us made us secure. Moving beyond those boundaries
can cause insecurity to arise. Boundaries are not merely
external things that delineate where one country ends and
another begins. Boundaries are also internal. Internal
boundaries are those assumptions we have held to be true
by virtue of the environment and culture we have been
raised in. Beliefs are often times culturally fostered. But a
belief or a philosophy of life for a certain group of people is
merely a set of assumptions upon which people base their
lives. Challenge the assumptions of an individual who has
adhered to them all his life and he becomes unsettled and
insecure. The problem, however, is that cultural philoso-
phies and assumptions are not necessarily true, even though
we believe them to be true, and even though we act as
though they are. Truth, if indeed it is truth, is universal.
Truth is not a philosophy, although one can be philosophical

about it. Truth is absolute and unchanging regardless of the country you were raised in.

When we first encounter the glory of God in truth, the assumptions we have held deeply within us are going to be confronted. In order to live in the fullness of God's glory therefore, we must shed the false assumptions that have been placed upon us both consciously and unconsciously as a result of our nationality, culture and ethnic background. All of these are internal limitations that hinder us from living in the expending consciousness of God's glory.

Not only was Abram to leave his country, he was to leave his relatives and his family. To leave the family is to leave the familiar. To leave the familiar is to move into the unfamiliar.

Abram was called by the glory of God to leave the familiar for that which was unfamiliar, namely, the glory of the Lord. To be familiar with what you are accustomed to is to be blind to that which you are unaccustomed. In order to see that which you are unaccustomed to seeing you must become blind to what you normally see. The glory of God would change Abram's perspective and vision, causing him to forsake the familiar in favor of what was not so. So says the prophet Isaiah of the ways of God's leading: "And I will lead the blind by a way in which they do not know, In paths they do not know I will guide them" (42:16).

To be blind is to be in need of security. The blind rely on the familiarity of the location in which they live. To place one who is blind in an unfamiliar location is to put them into a state of disease. We generally can only 'see' that which is familiar to us. That which is unfamiliar is usually something we are blind to. But such are the ways of the Lord. His glory hovers and broods in our lives to bring us from that with which we are all to familiar, living in lies and deception and limitation, in order to bring us to that which is most unfamiliar, namely the truth about God, about ourselves and about His purpose and destiny for our lives. The prophet goes on to say: "Who is so blind but My servant...as he that is at peace with Me" (42:19). To be the servant and messenger of the Lord is to become blind to what you once saw. It is becoming blind to the lie and the snare of the tempter and to be at total peace in the realm and the arena of truth, where the glory of the God rests and abides.

To leave the limitations and boundaries of what we once were identified with, and to leave the familiar for the unfamiliar is wonderful, but it is not enough in order to qualify for the inheritance of the saints of light and truth. Abram, as well as all of us, need also to leave our father's house. There are not merely cultural beliefs that are fostered within us from an early age, but there are also family beliefs and traditions, some of which are *cherishable*, others of which are *perishable.*

Traditions are not always beneficial. Family pressure can many times be the greatest hindrance to obeying God. But our love for God must be so great that our love for family by comparison seems to be as nothing. There is a certain part of our identity that is wrapped up in our natural parents and genealogy. Yet we are more than merely 'just like our parents'. People that grow up with that mindset never develop their uniqueness as individuals in life. Your uniqueness is what God created you for. Family traditions aren't necessarily worth laying your life down for. Traditions that family would want to pressure you with many times impinge on your destiny to become something more than your traditions have the ability to embrace. Prejudice is learned at home. Prejudice is far more than racial, it effects every area of our life. To enjoy the glory of God and live in the land He calls us to, it is necessary to leave our father's house. If we go reluctantly while still clinging in our hearts to anything from what we were raised under, we will ultimately have occasion to go back from whence we came.

To pursue the glory of God is to leave the limitations of our borders from their largest effect, whether it be race or nationality, to their smallest effect, being the things we have carried that are not true from our father's house.

It is as we are willing to go forth from all of these, that God begins to show a land unto us for which we are destined.

As is was with Abram, so it is with all of us, as the Cloud of Glory moves in our lives, it calls us out from our own limited assumptions, into the limitless possibilities linked with His glory. It remains therefore for us to do what we know needs to be done in order to be able to move with the Cloud wherever it goes.

In the words of the song:

Let your spirit arise, your strength be renewed.
Come let us move together.
As we follow where He leads, new life we will receive.
Move with the Cloud, move with the Cloud.

6

OUT OF THE COMFORT ZONE

When the Glory Cloud hovered over the original creation we are told that the earth was without FORM and void. The Glory Cloud came to deal with the problem of formlessness.

There is no longer a void, once form or pattern is established. Rather the pattern makes possible a resting place for the presence of God's glory.

Redemptive history moved from Abraham, to Isaac, to Jacob, and then to Joseph. Sold into slavery, Joseph prepares the way for his entire family's provision in Egypt, and ultimately the provision of the descendants of Jacob, the sons of Israel.

When Joseph died, he prophesied of the ultimate return of his people to the land of promise as it related to the Covenant his great grandfather had entered into with the

Lord. By faith he spoke of God's future provision and wanted his bones to be carried with the sons of Israel when God brought them out of Egypt.

The book of Exodus reveals the following information in the first chapter:

> Now a new king arose over Egypt, who did
> not know Joseph. (Ex.1:8)

Joseph was a man highly favored by Pharaoh and by the nation because of the blessing of the Lord upon his life. He was endowed with God-given wisdom and insight and proved invaluable to the economy of the nation. But when Pharaoh died, and Joseph died, the man who became Pharaoh not only did not know Joseph, nor Joseph's people, he did not know Joseph's God. He was insecure about the presence of a foreign body of people in his land. For him the only solution was to tyrannize them lest they become great in number and override his rulership.

God always moves through redemptive history in stages. Every climax in redemptive history comes at a very pregnant season. There is a *fullness of times* in the movings of God, and the stirrings of the Glory Cloud. The God who never lost dominion over the works of His hands, though he allowed man to operate within the sphere of his own volition, was about to accomplish a great act of redemption for their ungodly and pagan life-style of idolatry.

As with Abram, who needed to be brought out of the familiar into the unfamiliar by a revelation of the glory of the Living God, so God now had to burn all of the bridges built in His covenant nation that caused them to be attached to the life-style of Egypt. The sons of Israel were to be a separate people with a separate identity. Unlike the identity of other nations or peoples, the sons of Israel were in covenant with Jehovah God. They were to be a kingdom of priests unto Him.

After 400 years in Egypt, it was time to move with God into the further dimension of His restorational program. It wasn't the sons of Israel that were seeking God, it was God seeking them in spite of themselves.

But after a long period of history in a nation that had provided for them and gave them food, clothing and shelter in exchange for their labors, God was calling the sons of Israel to come out and be separate. Abraham was called to leave the familiar for the unfamiliar. Israel was called to leave the place of *comfort* for the place of *challenge*. Egypt had become convenient. It was a good place for the nation of Israel. But good is not necessarily good enough for the Lord. He wanted to call forth His people out of Egypt, causing them to give up the *good,* for the *best.*

To leave the comfort zone at times requires coaxing. Provocation is not always encouraging provocation. In the case of the old covenant nation, provocation came in the form of the ridiculous rulership of an insecure pharaoh. His fear drove him to tyrannize the nation. The tyrannizing of the nation brought tremendous affliction upon the people of God. Already whatever comforts Egypt had to offer, were being lost from sight in the sons of Israel. The provocation of Pharaoh was the very thing the Lord was going to use to bring Israel out of the comfort zone into the arena of challenge and adventure.

Provocation by Pharaoh led to supplication by the sons of Israel. Little did the sons of Israel realize that their supplication for deliverance from affliction was the very prayer God wanted to hear in order for Him to get their cooperation to bring them into the land of His purpose.

It was never the intention of God for the sons of Israel to remain in Egypt. But you cannot lead a people out from one place into another if they do not desire to be led. As with Adam in the garden, God wanted a man who chose to follow out of his own volition and love for God. God wanted to pull together an entire nation through whom He would fulfill His restorational purposes. He wanted them to walk in the unity of purpose that could accomplish such a task.

People are usually motivated to change when the need for change becomes evident. That is why the times and seasons of God are so important to understand. God brings things to their fullness before He brings forth the new things that He desires to do. In the case of the Israelites in Egypt, there had to come a fullness of times when they knew they could no longer remain in a land where the covenant God is dishonored. God had a particular place chosen for His purposes and a particular people through whom He could accomplish His Will.

The sons of Israel knew of the promise of God, and knew of His faithfulness to their father Abraham. But the promise of God requires fulfillment. Fulfillment requires cooperation. For God to accomplish all He intended, His people needed to walk with Him in the redemptive process. Their desire had to spur their motivation. Once they began to experience the persecution of Pharaoh in Egypt, the covenant nation began to cry out to God for deliverance. In their beseeching of God for deliverance, the covenant promise of a land was pregnant within them. But that pregnant desire had to grow to the point where it demanded a life of its own. That, in essence, is the FULLNESS. When a woman has carried a child to the full term of her pregnancy, that which was once a seed, has now taken on a life of its own, and outgrows the limited boundaries of the womb. It demands release and moves towards release. This is when travail comes upon a woman and the birth pangs of labor begin. So too, in the dealings of God, all dreams, desires, promises, must find their beginnings in God, Who plants the seed within the hearts of His people. As the seed of His Will grows, He begins to work in the outer circumstances to pave the way for the emergence of that new thing He is bringing about. At the point when that desire reaches its maturity and becomes capable of sustaining itself, the travail of affliction arises from the spirit of supplication and prayer and labor pains come upon the people of God as they are actually giving birth to a new move of God. Thus, in the fullness of times, God brings forth something new and vital which carries on His redemptive movement through this present age.

Under the Old Covenant, there was a fullness of times when God would not only judge Pharaoh, Egypt and all the gods of Egypt, but also bring His nation out of Egypt.

This was God's way of bringing to bear His sovereign working both in His own people as well as in those who were far from Him. Remember the Lord has always been King. He never lost His right to rule over the earth or the kingdoms of the earth, in spite of the deceitfulness of sin, and the serpent's power to deceive. God is still God.

God needs cooperation in order for visitation to be fruitful. Sovereign visitation cannot accomplish a great deal without human cooperation. In the fullness of time in that day, God raised up a man, who was rejected by his brethren. He was a man whose life was threatened at birth, but miraculously spared, and then raised in the very courts of Pharaoh. Moses was far removed from the affliction of his brethren. They had rejected him because he murdered the Egyptian. But he still could hear their cries though miles away in the desert, and absent for forty years from the intensity of the situation.

The wilderness has a way, however, of disorienting an individual. The vast changes in temperature, the heat of the noonday sun, the brutally cold nights, all have an effect on a man's outlook of reality. The loneliness, the lack of companionship and the relatively few people that live in the wilderness make for little conversation. The occasional merchant caravan crossing the desert affords an opportunity to catch up on life in the great cities of civilization. But as quickly as the merchants come, so quickly do they pass by and once again solitude becomes the only voice you hear.

Imagine the transition Moses went through from being favored to being a fugitive. He was a man without a city. Yet he, too, had to go through the process of being weaned from the familiar into the unfamiliar.

The Spirit makes plain for us the climax of this forty year transition in the man Moses:

> Now Moses was pasturing the flock of Jethro, his father-in-law, the priest of Midian, and he led the flock to the west side of the wilderness, and came to Horeb, the mountain of God. And the angel of the Lord appeared to him in a blazing fire from the midst of a bush, and he looked and behold the bush was burning with fire, yet the bush was not consumed. So Moses said, "I must turn aside now, and see this marvelous sight, why the bush is not burned up." When the Lord saw that he turned aside to look, God called him from the midst of the bush, and said, "Moses, Moses!" And he said, "Here I am."
> Then He said "Do not come near here; remove your sandals from your feet, for the place on which you are standing is holy ground."
> He said also, "I am the God of your father, the God of Abraham, the God of Isaac, and the God of Jacob." Then Moses hid his face, for he was afraid to look at God. (Exodus 3:1-6)

There are not many things to see on the back side of the wilderness that are uncommon. Moses had trekked through the sands of that region many times. For some reason, there was a rather large desolate mountain that had been referred to as the holy mountain of God. No one really knows for sure just why, but nevertheless, the Word calls it Horeb, the

MOUNTAIN OF GOD. Perhaps its size was somewhat more ominous than other mountains in that region. Yet it was not an uncommon looking peak. Mountains in Scripture have great significance. As a matter of fact, whenever the Glory Cloud appears in the Scripture, most often it appears on a mountain. Mountains in Scripture speak of kingdoms and realms of authority.

Life had its beginning on a mountain, at least if we believe the testimony of Scripture. In Ezekiel 28, the prophet takes up a taunt against the king of Tyre, a contemporary of Ezekiel, yet as you read the prophecy, it refers to someone quite other than one of Ezekiel's contemporaries.

If this is true that Eden was on the mountain of God, then it was at the heights of a mountain where the glory of God originally rested and abided. Therefore it would tie together with great consistency the many references in the Scripture to the restoration of the Mountain of the Lord, wherein would be established the house of the Lord, wherein would dwell the glory of the Lord.

The prophetic significance of the glory of God on a mountain therefore is of utmost importance in understanding that the purpose of God is Christ coming to "seek and save that which was lost".

Don't think it surprising, therefore, that when Moses happens upon this mountain, which is referred to as the mountain of God, that he should come in contact with the Glory Cloud in some particular manifestation. As always, when the Glory Cloud appears, contained within the Cloud is the fullness of heaven and the revelation of the government of God.

Man, however, as we have already stated in diverse ways, disoriented himself from the glory of God because of his alienation from the Lord. The glory of God therefore became most unfamiliar to man's experience.

In order for God to draw man out of the familiar in his own realm into the unfamiliar realm of the glory of God, God must get his attention by way of His glory. Before any great transition in Scripture, the Glory Cloud always appears. What was it that caused Abram to leave the familiar for the unfamiliar? It was the revelation of the glory of God. How would God get the attention of the man Moses? By a manifestation of His glory.

Moses was familiar with the desert. He was familiar with all of the characteristics of the life of the dessert. It would not have been *unfamiliar* for Moses to see a common bush burst into flames in the heat of the noonday sun. It was a common occurrence. In fact, so common was such a sight, that you would not pay much attention to such an event after seeing it happen often enough. I have no idea how long it would take for a bush to be consumed once the heat of the sun caused it to burst into flames. Perhaps a few seconds, perhaps a few minutes. On this occasion, however, that which was familiar and ordinary in the eyes of Moses, became strangely unfamiliar and extraordinary. The bush continued to burn and burn, and yet it was not consumed! There was not one branch on this dry bramble that was withering and disappearing. That which he initially judges as ordinary Moses now acknowledges as extraordinary. Isn't prejudicial thinking based on an already given set of judgements that we believe are true, even if they are false?

Through constant exposure to a given set of circumstances, Moses had already developed a judgement about reality. And to a certain degree he found it true. However, was what he believed really true? One of the tragedies of the fall is that man does not realize that life at the tree of the knowledge of good and evil lends itself to limitation and poor judgement of absolutes. It causes man to see only what he wants to see and nothing else. Isn't that what God told Isaiah to tell the nation of Israel?

Go and tell this people, 'Keep on LISTENING, but do not PERCEIVE, Keep on LOOKING, but do not UNDERSTAND.' Render the HEARTS of this people INSENSITIVE, Their ears DULL, and their eyes DIM. Lest they SEE with their eyes, HEAR with their ears, UNDERSTAND with their hearts, and return and be healed! (6:9-10)

What God is telling Isaiah is that because of the heart of man, he sees only what he wants to see because he only sees that which is consistent with what he personally believes to be true. That is what Jesus referred to when He told Nicodemus that you have to experience a new birth, a renaissance of revelation just to SEE the Kingdom (John 3:3). To be born from above requires a change of heart and a change of mind. That, in a nutshell, is REPENTANCE. It is the attitude of being willing to admit that what you are totally familiar with is not totally true and reliable. It involves touching us where all our pre-judged thinking lies, IN OUR HEARTS, and ALLOWING God to arrest our attention, as He did with Moses. This way He can show us an occurrence that heretofore we have always thought was one way, only to find at closer inspection, that things are not always as they appear.

The burning bush arrested the attention of the man Moses. It did not arrest his attention because it was burning, it arrested his attention because it was not consumed. At the moment when he made a decision to carefully consider the matter, he found himself in unfamiliar territory. "I must turn aside now to see..." That is what Moses said in his heart. I must turn aside NOW. That was a degree of repentance. To repent means to turn around, to change one's mind. God was about to expand the limited understanding of Moses. He is about to come into contact with the Glory Cloud. Once touched by it, he can no longer be the same. He will become converted to a new perspective of reality. A measure of restoration will take place in a mere man, because he has been overcome by the glory of God.

We are told that at the precise moment when Moses turned, God took notice and responded to his actions. God called to Moses. Moses first saw, and then he began to hear. God was restoring Moses' senses to their original intent, to respond to the SOUND OF HIS PRESENCE.

Not only does God open the eyes and ears of Moses to a wider perspective, but God also opens his heart. How? He calls him by name! That which (or rather, He who) Moses understands very little, understands him very well. God was introducing Himself to Moses. In calling his name, it was evident that he was known even though he knew not God. Consider the words of Paul: "However at that time when you did not know God, you were slaves to those which by nature are no gods. But now that you have come to know God, OR RATHER TO BE KNOWN BY GOD...(Gal. 4:8-9a).

In other words, God in encountering us, brings us to an awareness that we are known far better than we know ourselves. That opens our hearts to receive the light of truth in ever deepening ways, if we allow it to do so.

When God called Moses, he was not fully aware of what was transpiring, so he responded to his name by saying, "Here I am." Back in verse 2 we are told that the angel of the Lord appeared in the bush to Moses. Here too, we must accept the account of Holy Writ. It was a theophanic appearance. Though he SAW, he did not RECOGNIZE Who and what he saw. This, too, must be restored as far as God is concerned. There are many times when we can miss our day of visitation because we do not recognize His appearing. Sight does not necessarily imply recognition. Simeon the aged, had eyes that had been restored to see the glory of God, therefore, when the baby boy was brought in to the temple in the arms of His parents, that which was internally restored to his vision, became externally confirmed in the

Babe. He had eyes to see the day of his visitation from God. John tells us in the opening words of his gospel, that He (Christ) came to His own, and His own KNEW HIM NOT, and did not RECEIVE HIM (John 1:10-11).

When Adam fell, he caused mankind to fall into a state of becoming totally unfamiliar with the Presence of God. Even as the people of God, there are many times when God has visited us, and has manifested the glorious power of His Presence, and we have not been able to rightly discern the purpose for His visitation, and therefore have, at times, missed what He intended for us to not only SEE but RECOGNIZE.

But God in His grace, came to Moses for the purpose of giving Moses a revelation of Himself through the Glory Cloud. The greatest revelation a man can receive is a revelation of God Himself. All other revelation stems from that greatest of revelations.

In the process of this Divine encounter, God set the limits and boundaries for Moses. He was not to get too close. He was to remove his sandals. The ground upon which he stood was hallowed. What made it hallowed? God was there! The ground didn't look any different from any other ground, but God was there! God was right there where Moses stood. Man was intended to stand in the Presence of God's fullness without fear or shame.

In Eastern custom, sandals were removed in the presence of royalty. Moses was in the Presence of the King. He was on the King's Mountain. In all reverence and respect he was to humble himself and show honor by removing his sandals. He was not to bring the dust of the outer environment into the inner courtyard of the Royal Palace. Nothing of the world is allowed to defile the holy mountain of the Lord.

In reverence and respect, Moses removes his sandals. The Lord then reveals Himself as the God of the Covenant: The God of Abraham, Isaac, and Jacob. This too, was so unfamiliar to Moses. Surely he had heard about this God who appeared to Abraham. He had listened to his parents and the elders of Israel recount the dealings of God in the lives of the patriarchs. He himself worshipped this God, although he never KNEW Him. He was familiar with the accounts of the fathers with God, and perhaps on occasion something stirred in his heart to desire an encounter himself with the One Who cut covenant with Abraham. But being familiar with the story does not acquaint you with the Person. David says that Moses learned well of the Person, for while "He made known His acts to Israel, He made known of His WAYS to Moses" (Psa.103:7).

Moses was face to face with the Living God. How awesome. How overwhelming. How UNFAMILIAR. How unbelievable. The interesting thing though, is that at that moment of TRUTH, for TRUTH is a PERSON, Moses hid his face in fear. Why? Because in the Presence of TRUTH one must admit where he is. When face to face with God, Moses came face to face with himself and the guilt of the years as well as the reproach he felt in his heart for all that he thought he could do for his people, but failed to do. The reality of being a fugitive hurt. The wilderness he lived in resembled his own internal wilderness. It was all painfully evident there in the PRESENCE OF TRUTH HIMSELF. Had Moses really been running from Pharaoh all those years, or from a dead Egyptian soldier, or perhaps from himself? In the encounter at Horeb, Moses had to stop running. Once he stopped, provision was made there for his guilt and his fear, for he found no condemnation in the Presence of God, only the opportunity to find grace to be of service to the King! Even when he tried to disqualify himself because of his distorted view of who he was, God refused to hear his excuses. God had arrested a man by His glory and reoriented him in order that He might accomplish an additional stage in the consummation of His purposes.

7

FIRST THE NATURAL THEN THE SPIRITUAL

In considering the flow of redemptive history from the fall to the birth of Christ and thereafter, it becomes evident that God began the work of restoration over long periods of time because of man's alienation. God worked by way of externals in order to convey spiritual truth to a people disoriented to the inner dimension of reality.

As wonderful as the types and shadows of the Old Covenant were, they were merely types and shadows. They pointed to a dimension of reality that was in a coming day. They spoke symbolically and parabolically of "that which was lost".

God's program of recovery was very carefully planned out over the generations of history to bring things into absolute focus in the fullness of times.

Moses was the answer to the prayers of the sons of Israel. God would use him as the instrument to bring His people out of bondage and prepare them to become a habitation of God. God desired a place for His Kingdom to come in fullness on earth as it was in heaven. He never deviated from that intent. He wanted a people to be formed to house His glory in all its absolute fullness. In a very real sense mankind now resembled the formless void of Genesis 1. From God's perspective He moved to bring man back to a proper foundational understanding of his source of origin as well as destiny. God is the cause behind every effect.

Mankind, in his fallen state, was formless, without pattern and therefore void of the ability to contain the Presence of His glory. God moved covenantally in order to restore that which was lost. In spite of man's rebellion, God's covenant love caused Him to not forsake His highest creation, the human race, created by Him to be His dwelling place. Eventually it must dawn on our consciousness that while some of us are so busy trying to get to heaven, God is at work to get heaven into us. The one is religious humanism, the other is the other is the ultimate purpose of God for His sons.

When Moses brought the children of Israel out, they were brought to the foot of the very Mount of revelation where Moses left all that was familiar behind. There at the mount the same Glory Cloud that arrested his attention now comes down over the entire mountain before the eyes of the entire nation.

There God once again moves according to the original Edenic pattern. The account reads this way:

Then Moses went up to the mountain, and the cloud covered the mountain. And the *glory of the Lord* RESTED on Mount Sinai, and the cloud covered it SIX DAYS; and on the SEVENTH DAY He called Moses from the midst of the cloud. And to the eyes of the sons of Israel the appearance of the glory of the Lord was

like a consuming fire on the mountain top. And Moses
entered the midst of the cloud as he went up to the
mountain; and Moses was on the mountain forty days
and forty nights. (Ex. 24:15-18)

It is evident that God is abiding by the original six day
pattern where the Glory Cloud brooded and hovered until
the formless void took a form that matched what was in the
heart of God, and when that was completed God came down
and rested in the garden.

So too, the Glory Cloud now covers the mount for six days.
During that time God is absolutely silent. It is not until the
Sabbath day, the seventh day, that Moses hears the voice out
of the cloud calling him to come up a little higher.

During that time Moses sat or knelt in silence watching,
waiting and worshipping the Lord. Though man fell, and
something was lost, God never again spoke out of anything
but Sabbath REST. For His works were completed from
before the foundation of the world.

When Moses heard the Lord call on the seventh day, it was
then that God revealed the pattern of the heavenly tabernacle where He chose to dwell. The command He then gave
to Moses the architect was this: "And let them construct a
sanctuary for Me, that I may DWELL among them.
According to all that I am going to show you, as the
PATTERN of the tabernacle and the pattern of all its
furniture, JUST SO shall you construct it" (25:8-9).

Please notice that the heart of God to dwell with His
people is ever evident. But it says "DWELL AMONG". That
is all shadow and not substance. God's ultimate purpose is to
DWELL WITHIN. But it required the fullness of times for
that to occur. Yet even in shadow, it had to be done JUST SO
as the Lord had said. The implications are clear: if the
sanctuary is not constructed JUST SO, God will not choose
to REST in it.

According to Exodus 40, the work indeed was done according to pattern:

> Thus Moses finished the work. Then the CLOUD covered the tent of meeting, and the GLORY of the Lord FILLED the tabernacle. And throughout all their journeys whenever the cloud was taken up from over the tabernacle the sons of Israel would set out; but if the cloud was not taken up, then they did not set out until the day when it was taken up. For throughout all their journeys, the Cloud of the Lord was on the tabernacle by day, and there was fire in it by night, in the sight of all the house of Israel. (40:33b-38)

God was pleased with the pattern and then occupied that portion where He chose to dwell in all His FULLNESS. He FILLED the tent of meeting!

These verses in Scripture are inspiring and cause our hearts to soar at what it must have been like. But beloved, there is so much more than what Moses could offer. It seems tragic that so many of God's people find tremendous solace in the shadows, when they miss the LIGHT OF DAY that has come in Christ. All of these types were just types. They were externals. God was moving from without because of the alienation and disorientation of man. His intent, however, was to restore what was lost INTERNALLY to man. As glorious as the shadows are, they fall short of the fullness of God's glory. They were merely the shadow of good things to come.

Even the temple of Solomon, when completed and dedicated during the Feast of Tabernacles (2 Chronicles 5:7-ff), was merely a shadow of good things to come. Even one hundred and twenty priests blowing trumpets in unison with the entire congregation exclaiming the covenant grace of God cannot continue when the Cloud of Glory descends because of the overwhelming Majesty of His glory.

But it wasn't all that many centuries or even decades later when the nation began to decline and the glory departed and even that temple was destroyed and the people were carried away into captivity.

The great theme of the prophets was that God would restore His house and fill it with His GLORY! Many years later under the prophetic inspiration of Haggai, another temple was erected. And on the day when the Feast of Tabernacles began, the greatest of all the celebrations of the Old Covenant nation, he stands and prophesies to the people of God that the latter glory of that house would be greater than the former glory of Solomon's house. (Haggai 2:9). Peter tells us that the prophets of old "made careful search and inquiry, seeking to know what manner of time the Spirit of Christ within them was indicating as He predicted the suffering of Christ and the GLORIES to follow. It was revealed that they were not serving themselves, but YOU, in these things which NOW have been announced to you by those who preached the GOSPEL to you by the Holy Spirit sent from heaven" (I Peter 1:11-12).

The latter glory of the temple that Haggai prophesied over never saw the visitation that Solomon's temple had. But was his word therefore invalid? Not at all. Haggai was seeing something far beyond his present day and by the Spirit spoke of the restoration of that which was lost from God's original intention.

Haggai prophesied of the shaking of both heavenly and earthly things, and of then the shaking of the nations, and then total restoration of God's glory in all the earth.

We lose a great deal of understanding in this day and age when we endeavor to understand the words of the prophets with a 20th century or 21st century mindset. Haggai was not speaking of the literal earth or the literal heaven, nor was Joel literally speaking of the sun, moon and stars being darkened before the great and terrible day of the Lord.

The prophets often spoke out of the shadows using symbols common to the people then alive to convey things that were more than EXTERNALS. The prophets prophesied of a spiritual dimension, an inner dimension that would ultimately accomplish for God that which He originally intended.

Joseph dreamed of the sun, moon and stars and it represented the twelve tribes of Israel. The Old Covenant nation was never intended to be the final event. It was intended to carry the oracles of the mysteries of God until the fullness of times and then release that which was entrusted to them for the purpose of seeing the earth filled to all the fullness of the Glory of the Lord.

Haggai said that God was going to shake all that could be shaken. The writer of the book of Hebrews sheds light for us on what Haggai prophesied about. In Hebrews twelve the writer of the epistle speaks of the unshakeable Kingdom of God. But in the process he reminds his readers that all earthly systems would be shaken, and even heavenly things would experience a time of shaking. To whom was the writer to the Hebrews addressing his exhortation? He was addressing his words to Hebrew believers, who left the earthly, Old Covenant system of laws, rituals and offerings for something greater. They left the shadows for what had come in Christ as substance. They left the external dimension for the internal dimension. But now because their own brethren by birth were persecuting them and threatening their lives, they wanted to forsake the REAL and go back to live under the shadow. They were retreating to externals.

They were not able to comprehend the words of the prophets, when they spoke of the shaking of the earthly system. The word in Hebrews says that the purpose of the shaking was for the "removing of things which can be shaken" (v. 27). That word *removing* is a word which means to be carried from one place to another. The idea implies making a transition. Some of us lose our footing in transition, we lose our perspective. The reason that happens is because we don't understand the purpose of transition. Transition is for the shaking off of the externals to prepare us to come into the fullness of internal reality. Transition is intended by God to carry us from the familiar into the unfamiliar. It is the place of shedding old wineskins for the sake of new wine and new wineskins.

Something in man causes him to become secure in externals. Religious works appease a conscience that is constantly trying to work its way to God. As hard as man tries, his works will never get him BACK TO THE GARDEN. It is the work of God to bring us back to Himself.

The system of laws and rituals for the observance of externals served to only convey a message that there was more to come. Yet in seeing they could not see. The people missed the intent of the prophets because they placed their own interpretation based on externals. They made a judgement based on accumulated data. This is the essence of prejudice. Their accumulated data was incomplete, because God had not revealed, since the fall, the fullness of His purposes. They were living under the light of the moon. All the Old covenant festivals were ordered around the moon. The Day of the Lord was not come until the dawning of the light of the sun. The Hebrew day according to prophetic pattern began in the evening dusk. There was EVENING and morning the first day (Gen. 1:5). The Hebrew day began at 6 P.M.. So also all the feasts of Israel began on the EVE of the SABBATH. The Old Covenant nation lived in the evening of the day. The light of the moon is wonderful, but it is only a reflection. It is not so totally illuminating that all objects are clear and visible. In the full light of day things appear quite differently. The shadows that moonlight casts can make objects appear quite differently than they really are. The prophets struggled with their revelations from God, because they were looking from the perspective of the evening light. The day was yet to dawn. It is not good to make absolute judgements when darkness looms overhead. When the fullness of light comes, clarity is then given.

Unfortunately, history makes clear that for many of the nation of Israel alive at the dawning of the day, they rejected the light. Christ came to His own, but their prejudice caused them to prejudge all things by their limited scope and perspective. They refused the grace that showed them where they really were. They would rather have the externals. Moses was good enough.

But as good as Moses was, as wonderful as the Tabernacle was, it was only a shadow. It was incapable of making man perfect. Man's idea of perfection falls far short of God's idea. Is it any wonder why? Man judges perfection from his limited concept of what it is. Until he is willing to let the Cloud of Glory bring him through transition it will be impossible to understand what God is really after. Man's pride won't allow the truth to penetrate that deeply. He is secure in the externals because externals leave him free to rule his own internal environment. But from the beginning, God's government was to be internal and impartational. To become all God intends for man to become, he must rely on God, and not on his concepts. Externals enable man to keep God in abeyance and hold Him at a distance. God has no distant relatives. He only has sons (editorially speaking).

The law cannot make man perfect. The law reveals how imperfect one really is. Perfection only comes through the grace of impartation. Perfection is not a doctrine it is a PERSON!

8

THE RESTORATION OF THE HOUSE OF THE LORD

The prophets continually spoke of the house of the Lord. Their concern was for God's reputation in the earth. God's glory was at the heart of their ministry. All of the prophets take up the theme of the house of the Lord being restored to its fullness. But what was the house of the Lord? Was the house the Tabernacle or the Temple?

David had a great love for the HOUSE of the Lord. The sweet psalmist of Israel constantly sang variations on that theme:

I will dwell in the HOUSE of the Lord forever. (23:6)
O Lord I love the habitation of Thy HOUSE, and the place where Thy GLORY dwells (26:8)

> ...that I may dwell in the HOUSE of the Lord all the days of my life... (27:4)
> Zeal for Thy HOUSE has consumed me... (69:9)
> How blessed are those who dwell in Thy HOUSE, they are ever praising Thee! (84:4)

The house of the Lord is the place where the Father lives. Father did not dwell in the outer court of the Tabernacle or of the Temple. Neither did He dwell at the laver of ceremonial washing. Nor did the Father dwell in the Holy Place where one could find the Lampstand, the Table of Shewbread and the Altar of Incense. Father dwelt in one place and one place only. The particular place that was known as His HOUSE was the sanctuary, the set-apart place, unable to be entered by man. Father dwelt in the HOLY OF HOLIES.

Isn't it interesting that although God dwelt among them, the distance between them was still great. It was all indeed because of the fall. As the cherubim originally guarded the way to the Tree of Life and the glory of God, so too, in the most holy place they sat over the ark guarding God's glory.

None were allowed into Father's House. It was only on the Day of Atonement that the High Priest would be allowed into Father's Presence to offer the blood of the lamb atoning for the sins of a rebellious and obstinate people.

But there had to be a Day of Atonement year after year to satisfy the demands of justice. No matter how much blood was shed, Father's House was off limits to all.

Built into the eternal system of the Law with its priesthood and sacrifices was a God-ordained intention of despair. The Law reveals God's utter holiness and our absolute alienation from Him. The Law could not make one perfect enough to have access back into the GARDEN OF GOD. To be fully restored required being brought back into Edenic Glory.

The prophets prophesied of a day when such a thing would be reality. They longed for it and cried out for it. They died never seeing it.

Yet in the fullness of time a day would dawn, the day when the seed of the woman would come forth as the Conqueror. Upon Him would be conferred the dominion of the ages. He would be entrusted with rulership of the earth. He would deal with Adam's fall, the serpent's lie, the woman's anguish, and bring man back to God's HOUSE. He would restore man to the GARDEN OF EDEN.

When the children of Israel cried out for release from bondage Moses was able to take them out of Egypt. But he was not able to take Egypt out of them. There is something in man that lends itself to alienation from God. The Law could not, by a series of externals, save man from his own bent at self-destruction and death. Death reigned from Adam. Death reigned even while Moses ministered over the affairs of the Father. The need in the sons of Israel was to see that they had more of a need than they realized.

Something needed to arise as a prayer out of their innermost being that said "SAVE US". Save us from what? From ourselves. Bring us back to the garden. We have tried to return and yet the flaming sword has prevented our access. No matter how much blood is offered on our behalf it is insufficient to cleanse the conscience from evil. The tree of death has imparted a death consciousness to our entire being.

God, we need to see how blind we really are. Save us from our destruction. There is something within us that prevents us from living in Your fullness.

Those that truly understood that, lived and died travailing for its day. Abraham died in faith, as did Moses, Joseph, Jacob, Jeremiah, Isaiah, Daniel, Zechariah, and all the prophets.

Visitation from God was wonderful. But they longed for HABITATION! They had limited visiting rights into His house. They vicariously visited Father's House once a year on the breastplate of their High Priest. When he went into

Father's House, they were included in his visit. But it wasn't the same as being there.

Still, there was a tremendous fear about being there. It was the same fear that Adam knew the moment he fell. His guilt caused him to fear the wrath of the King. So too, that fear gripped the hearts of all the people under the Cloud in the wilderness. Even Moses said the sight was so awesome that he himself, who talked to God face to face, was full of fear and trembling (Deut. 9:19).

It was a fearful thing to enter within the veil and offer the blood of the sacrifice, for if God was not pleased with the sacrifice, the High Priest would lose his life in the process. For that reason they tied a rope around his ankle in the event that he was judged for their sin. They would then have to pull him out by the rope.

The Law had a built in futility. Why? Because as Paul tells us in Galatians, it was given to be a tutor that would DRIVE US to Christ. It showed man that the only way he could run from God was to run to God. The One who judges also held the secret of mercy. Man needed a Deliverer.

> What does Scripture say?
>
> Sacrifice and meal offering Thou hast not desired;
> My ear Thou hast opened;
> Burnt offering and sin offering Thou hast not required.
> Then I said, "Behold I come; in the scroll of the book it is written of ME;
> *I delight to do Thy will, O my God;*
> *Thy law is WITHIN my heart."* (Psalm 40:6-8).

Restoration required a Man, who when given the same opportunities Adam had, would make the right choice instead of the wrong one, and by His obedience bring justification to the lost. There is only problem. Sin has become a part of mankind internally. All the sons of Adam had been given the same impartation of his sin through the bloodline. How can a man be born without sin? God Himself would have to take on the form of Man and become the Intercessor for Adam's race.

Somehow this Glory Cloud that had brooded over the original creation and brought a pattern into existence, and then after the fall brooded over a people to bring them into existence, now must brood once again. The brooding this time, however, cannot be on the external system. The brooding must now begin at the internal level. In order for a Man without sin to be born, there needs to be a restoration of the Inner Dimension. A man must be born who, like Adam when created, KNEW NO SIN.

All of history would find its centrality at that pivotal point in the economy of God. For what would be true of that man, should He succeed in accomplishing His purpose, would usher in a new age in which mankind could move from the external dimension to the inner dimension. He would pick up where Adam fell, and ultimately take dominion over the earth under the government of God. Man would ultimately fill the earth with the fullness of His Glory.

9

THE ULTIMATE VISITATION

"And behold, you will conceive in your womb, and bear a son, and you shall name Him Jesus. He will be great, and will be called the Son of the Most High; and the Lord God will give Him the throne of His father David; and He will reign over the house of Jacob forever; and His kingdom will have no end. And Mary said to the angel, 'How can this be, since I am a virgin?' And the angel answered and said to her, 'The Holy Spirit will COME UPON YOU, and the power of the Most High will OVERSHADOW YOU; and for that reason the holy offspring shall be called the SON OF GOD.'" (Luke 1:31-35).

The Incarnation is the pivotal point of history in the plan of God. John tells us in his gospel that "the WORD became FLESH and DWELT AMONG US, and we beheld His

GLORY'' (1:14). Of all the marvelous sights to see in the temple of Solomon, with its ornate furnishings and decor, and of all the intricacies of the Tabernacle of Moses, with its precise detail to fulfill the pattern shown Moses on the Mount, the Incarnate Word becomes the epitome of the Glory Pattern. Christ is the perfect expression of the Will of the Father. Christ is the One who expresses in totality the Will of God in His desire for His Kingdom to come on earth even as it is in heaven.

When the writer to the Hebrews opens his letter, he begins by making an amazing description of the same Glory Cloud pattern revealed in Genesis: "And He is the radiance of His Glory, and the EXACT REPRESENTATION of His nature, and upholds all things by the word of His power." Christ is the Pattern. He is the Pattern Temple and the Pattern Son. The effulgence of the brooding Cloud of Glory finds its fullest expression in Him. He expresses the throne, the government and the power and glory of the Father. He more than expresses, He embodies it all. In Him is the fullness of God.

The process of redemption was a delicate thing. All things had to be done in a manner which would speak of the justice of God. It was man who was created to be His co-ruler. It was man who by willful disobedience relinquished his right to rule, and therefore it requires a MAN to restore all that was lost. So Paul makes it plain when he declares that: "when the FULLNESS of times came, God sent forth His SON, BORN OF A WOMAN, BORN UNDER THE LAW, in order that He might redeem those who were under that Law, that we might receive the adoption as sons" (Gal. 4:4-5).

Christ, the agent of the First Creation, now becomes the agent of the New Creation. By His life, death and resurrection, He will cause all things that are true of Him to be true of all those who are created anew in His Likeness and Image.

Please consider the similarities between His birth and the original pattern in Genesis. Mary was a virgin and could not understand how she would conceive without knowing a man. The angle made clear how God would accomplish such a task. The Holy Spirit would come upon her. There had to be a descent from heaven of the Spirit of God even as at the beginning. Not only would it come down upon her but it would OVERSHADOW her. The word here describes very much the same idea as the word Moses used to describe the brooding of the Glory Cloud. The picture being of an eagle spreading its wings over her young to bring them on to maturity. The incubation period under the cloud that would bring into existence the "Let there be" that was spoken by God and delivered by the angel.

The end result of the activity of the Spirit upon her would produce a Holy Offspring. A pure Seed, without the taint of sin. In every way He would be in the same pristine innocence that Adam was before he fell.

Never had anyone lived as Jesus did. During the thirty years of His preparation for His public ministry, we are told in the gospel that He "increased in wisdom and stature and in favor with both God and men". Adam was called to transform innocence into holiness by a series of choices. The more he made the right decisions, the more he would increase in wisdom and stature in God. Jesus from the time He was a child consistently chose to do the Will of God. He continually chose to partake of the Tree of Life. He always knew perfectly the Will of the Father. Every time the tempter came to Him, He chose to cultivate and keep the Garden of God in His life. He limited Himself to grow and learn as a human being, in like manner to all of us. This is not to deny the Divinity of Christ for He was fully Divine. Yet the Scriptures make plain that He emptied Himself, and took the form of a bond servant and as a MAN under the government of the Glory Cloud, overcame by obedience and reliance on the Spirit of God.

To put Jesus into an arena where all the works of power He did, or His defeat of the enemy, were the result of His being God, would totally make void the purpose of His coming, and the process of redemption.

Jesus the Man overcame the devil, and Jesus the Man took dominion according to Genesis 1:26 in all that He accomplished. When God gave man dominion, He did not give him dominion over other men. Man was never intended to have dominion over other men or even women for that matter. God created each to be unique expression of His grace and glory. Man's only dominion in relation to flesh and blood was to learn by a series of choices to rule himself! That was what caused Adam to fall. It was not the devil, it was Adam's failure to take dominion over his own feelings and desires and submit them to a loving God who had promised to more than take care of all his needs.

Can this be proven? Absolutely. Consider for a moment the temptation of Jesus in the wilderness in Matthew four. The temptation comes immediately following His baptism by John in the Jordon. When Jesus arrived at the Jordan to be baptized by John, John tried to hinder Him. But Jesus stressed the fact that it was necessary for Him to be baptized in order to fulfill all righteousness. What kind of righteousness was Jesus speaking of? He had committed no sin, nor injustice. He never knew what sin was. He was a perfect Man. What then was necessary in His baptism? His baptism was totally unlike ours. When we are baptized we identify with His death, burial and resurrection. When He was baptized, He was entering into the full implications of our fallen humanity. In doing so, He would be able to be a High Priest who would be touched with the feeling of our infirmities.

Here the Messiah has come to the very day of His public appearing. From all indications in Scripture, His growth in wisdom and stature was based on His ever increasing understanding by the Word and the Spirit of Who He was. He had intuitively heard the voice of the Father in the Word by the Spirit. Now at His baptism He is identifying with His life's call to die for a sinful and fallen race. That was an act of obedience by the Lord. After being baptized, He comes up out of the water, and once again the Glory of God descends with wings in the form of a dove and rests upon Him. We are told that He received the Spirit without measure. As it was on the day of dedication of the Tabernacle of Moses, and as it was on the day of dedication of the temple of Solomon, so on the day of dedication of that which would be the prototype of the New Creation, the Cloud of Glory descends and fills the Temple named Jesus. And at that point there comes an external confirmation of an internal reality. Jesus has lived by internals because the pattern was fleshed out in Him. But now, He receives an external confirmation. The voice of the Father giving approval to the Pattern Son. Here was the affirming hand of God setting His seal of approval on His Son, not because of what He did but because of Who He WAS. In other words, He embodied truth, and such was well pleasing unto the Father. Adam never had the joy of that experience of affirmation, and thus was driven by a constant fallen concept that his performance would cause him to regain his approval and affirmation with God.

This, too, is the dilemma of so many in the Church. We believe that if we try just a little harder we will gain God's approval. Approval does not come because of what we can do. We already showed ourselves for what we are in Adam.

If we could have performed our way to God's approval what need would there have been for the Son of Man to come and seek and save that which was lost? Religious humanism is nothing new, it began with Adam. There is only one life that has ever pleased the Father. He is always ready to live again through us the moment we stop trying to perform in our own strength to get His approval.

Once the affirmation came to Jesus we are told that the Spirit literally drove Him into the wilderness for the express purpose of being tempted by the devil. Matthew 4:1-11 gives us a blow by blow account of the entire ordeal. But the temptation in the wilderness settles once and for all the issue of what dominion is all about. Dominion boils down to God's man taking control over himself. We are not called to rule others. We are called to posses our own souls. How would it be possible to lead another if we ourselves have not been able to rule over our own lives?

When temptation came in the garden, Adam had every convenience the garden had to afford. When the tempter came to Adam and Eve, to entice them to eat of the wrong tree, there were so many other trees in view that he could have simply found one which God approved of to satisfy his need. But when Jesus was tempted He was not given all that, because it was not there to be given. Adam had seen to that by his disobedience. In addition, Jesus had fasted forty days and forty nights. Forty is always number implying TRANSITION in Scripture. He too was in transition, not for Himself, but for us. It wasn't until after He had already fasted forty days, that the tempter came. The enemy came to Jesus at His weakest point. He was hungry. True hunger, we are told by medical experts, does not set in until after body has gone without food for 40 days. It takes forty days of fasting before the body totally eliminates all toxins, and all reserve supplies of energy and food, and then the body begins to consume itself. Jesus was hungry. What better opportunity for the tempter to entice? Yet this was allowed and ordained of God for a purpose. Remember, He came to seek and save that which was lost. When the devil came to tempt Him, he said "IF YOU ARE THE SON OF GOD..."

Now it seems obvious that Jesus knew Who He was. He Himself heard both internally and even externally that the Father referred to Him as His Beloved Son. But the issue of being God's Son was not the issue here. Jesus replied to the devil when told to turn stones into bread that "MAN shall not live by bread alone, but by the PROCEEDING WORD OF GOD." Jesus does not move out of the realm of being a MAN under the government of God. As a man, He cannot rely on some hocus pocus to satisfy His own needs. The last thing He heard from Father was that it was time to fast and be put to the test. That was the proceeding word to Him. Until God showed up again, He would trust Him for His provision. Adam didn't obey God's proceeding word, and when the tempter came, he ignored the Word of the Lord, and sought to satisfy himself independently of covenant relationship with the Father.

Jesus has looked intently into the perfect law of liberty, and not forgetting Who He was, a MAN under God's government, He chose to be an effectual doer of the Word. He maintained dominion over His own appetite. Thus the devil lost round one.

When the devil takes Him to the pinnacle of the temple he pulls verses out of context from Psalm 91 in an effort to get Jesus to announce in some supernatural way that He indeed was the Messiah. If you really are like God, jump off and prove it. For sure every one will see that such a spectacular event proves You are the Messiah! Once again, Jesus already knew Who He was. He did not have to prove Who He was. As a MAN under the government of God, He had no ambition to be like God, therefore His only ambition was to walk in the parameters of the Will of the Father. He wouldn't dare think of abusing God's power or encroach on His integrity to force the hand of God. Satan lost round two to a MAN who knew self-control and took dominion.

The devil saved the coup-de-gras for round three. He took Jesus to a great and high MOUNTAIN. Interesting that he had to go the heights of a mountain. It was more than a place of advantage for the purpose of seeing what he showed Him. When Lucifer rebelled, his internal ambition was to ascend above the stars of God (Isa.14). He wanted to sit on the heights of the mountain of God in the recesses of the north. That pride led to his own demise. He never made it to the mountain. God cast him down. In a moment in time the devil showed Jesus all the kingdoms of the world. He then interjects that they are his to give to whomever he wishes. Since that is the case then Jesus, just fall down and worship me once, and you can rule with me. It is critical at this point to ask the question, "Does the devil tell the truth?" Jesus made it clear later on that he was a liar from the beginning. When Adam fell, who lost? Did God? We have already established the fact that God did not lose a thing. It was Adam who lost rulership over himself and the works of God's hands. Adam lost the power to take dominion over the elements and the animal kingdom and the like. But whose kingdom is it anyway? The devil can talk about all the kingdoms of the world he wants to, they really are not kingdoms at all. There is only ONE TRUE KINGDOM, all the other kingdoms are temporal. God's Kingdom is the EVERLASTING KINGDOM and His SOVEREIGNTY RULES OVER ALL. This temptation of the devil was the biggest lie of all. Should Jesus have even bowed once, do you really think the devil would have delivered the goods? The devil promised Adam and Eve quite a future. Did he deliver? Of course not, because he is a liar and has nothing to deliver but a lie. How foolish and ignorant for the tempter to presume to have rulership of the world to offer to Jesus. But he was desperate, he has already lost two rounds. If he just gets Jesus to worship him once, all will be settled. Man will give everything in exchange for his soul. Not so with the

MAN Christ Jesus. There was only One King in His eyes, and only One Kingdom and only One God and One Lord. He alone was worthy of worship and service. He had already been promised rulership of the whole earth in eternity past by His Father. His Father was holding it in trust. Sorry satan, you are a cheep liar and you are worthless to Me. Get BEHIND ME. Church, when Jesus said GET BEHIND ME it was all over for satan. The issue of Calvary was settled there once and for all. The enemy lost hold totally and completely as far as Jesus was concerned. He was defeated at that point. The prince of the world had nothing in the Son of Man. Now, in the power of the Spirit, the Pattern Son would begin by His having taken dominion over Himself in obedience to the proceeding word of God, begin to tear down the strongholds of the liar. He would begin to destroy the works of the devil. Hallelujah! The issue was settled. God found a MAN Whom He could entrust with dominion and authority, for He was under authority. The MAN took dominion over the fish of the sea. "Drop your nets on the right side of the boat" (Luke 5). It doesn't matter how long you fished all night, I am under the government of God, therefore according to Genesis 1:26 I have dominion over the fish of the sea. There's a big catch that I have appointed to fall into the nets. Take My Word for it!

The elements? What challenge to a Covenant Man do they offer? He was content to sleep in the storm in Mark 4:35-ff. It wasn't the storm that woke up Jesus, it was the frightened disciples! Once aroused, being a Man under authority, He took dominion over the contrary winds, behind which was the sinister spirit of the age, and then commanded the sea to be still. Satan had to obey God's Man, because he had nothing in Him legally to usurp His authority.

Do you get the picture? Jesus the Man, the Perfect Pattern, embodies the Word. He embodies the Creative

Word of God. He lives and breathes the Word for He is the Word. What can stand against the Word of the Lord?

To such a MAN, God would entrust all the works of His hands, and joyfully take pleasure in His Son taking dominion. In Christ we discover the heart of God in all its fullness. Christ becomes the Head of a new RACE. He would father a new line of men and women. A redeemed mankind, restored to the place of rulership in God as a result of being able, by His death and burial and resurrection; to exercise dominion over sin. Sin shall no longer have dominion over you, at least that was the gospel Paul preached. If a man in Christ can rule himself, he can also do the things Jesus did, and even greater things. Why? In Jesus ascending to the Father, He established a NEW Covenant. A Covenant with an INNER DIMENSION. God by His Spirit would write the LAW OF LIBERTY on the HEARTS OF RIGHTEOUS MEN MADE PERFECT BY THE FINISHED WORK OF CHRIST. All the miracles Jesus performed as Man under the government of God, were done in fulfillment of the Old Covenant. Healing and deliverance were part of the Old Covenant promise. In fulfilling the Old, Jesus then removes it by His death. In His resurrection He establishes a NEW and BETTER COVENANT. When did Jesus go to the Father? After the resurrection. Therefore, having entered into the Heavenly Holy of Holies, He abides a High Priest of a BETTER COVENANT, He will never die. He abides a PRIEST PERPETUALLY by a new order. That is a NEW COVENANT. GREATER WORKS are to be done under the NEW COVENANT. I am not quite convinced that we have seen the greater works, at least not in their fullness. We still struggle over healing and deliverance. And we need to learn how to minister in such areas to the oppressed and the downtrodden. But it is my conviction that there is a realm over which we have yet to understand how to fully take dominion. The weather, the animal kingdom, famines and the like are areas and realms in which the Church has a destiny.

The key, perhaps, is to learn to take dominion over ourselves. For too long we have been trying to run the lives of others. God never gave us the right to rule over the lives of others. He has called us to rule over ourselves through the NEW LAW, the Law of Liberty. The law of the Spirit of Life in Christ Jesus.

Proverbs 16:32 makes this commentary: "He who is slow to anger is better than the mighty, and he who RULES HIS SPIRIT, than he who CAPTURES A CITY." The amazing thing about this verse is that Jesus fulfilled the first part. He was slow to anger, He ruled His Spirit. Isn't it interesting that as a result He was given a CITY, and even more than a CITY. The kingdoms of this world are become the Kingdom of our Lord and of His Christ and HE SHALL REIGN FOREVER AND EVER.

The inner dimension in Jesus becomes the pattern for the New Creation. He is the LION of JUDAH for surely He has conquered the enemies of God. But He learned dominion by being the Lamb of God. There is a Lamb on the throne. The Spirit hovered over the Creation to find a resting place but never found one in permanence. But in Christ the dove rested and remained, for the Pattern was perfect. There was a Lamb in Lion's clothing. Jesus was a MAN in full submission to the government of God, and thus was given the right to rule. "The Scepter shall not depart from Judah, until SHILOH comes, and to Him shall be given the RIGHT to rule" (Genesis 49:10).

10

SUMMING UP ALL THINGS IN CHRIST

Jesus answered and said to them, "Destroy this temple and in three days I will raise it up." The Jews therefore said, "It took forty-six years to build this temple (more literally: This temple has been in the process of being built for forty-six years, and is still unfinished), and You will raise it up in three days?" But He was speaking of the temple of His body. (John 2:19-21).

On many occasions Jesus spoke things that were hard to understand. Especially for the legalists and literalists. The Pharisees had such a difficult time with Jesus. In the account read above, Jesus has just cleansed the temple of thieves and robbers, and they questioned His authority. They asked for a sign of His right to do such a thing. Isn't it interesting that they didn't get really angry or in the common vernacular terribly bent-out-of shape by His actions to the point of doing Him harm? At least not in this instance. The Pharisees knew full well the corruption that went on at Passover, when people had to pay high prices for a sacrifice. They who ran the temple allowed corruption to go on in the Name of the Lord.

It wasn't uncommon in Jesus' day for a man and his family to travel a great distance to be part of the Passover celebration in obedience to Deuteronomy 16. Each man would often bring his lamb with him from home. He had to be sure it was a lamb without spot or blemish, for it was Passover. His lamb would have to pass inspection by the priests in order to be offered. Oftentimes the priests would be in league with the money changers and the merchants who sold sheep for the Passover. If they wanted to make money, they would inspect the lamb, and say it was not good enough. After taking it from the family, they would be forced to buy one of theirs. They, in turn, would eventually sell yours to someone else. Jesus had good reason to be angry. It is interesting that all the Pharisees could say to Him was, "Give us a 'sign' to prove You have the authority to do what You are doing." If they saw a sign they would have been satisfied, which means they were aware of the illegality of the practice, but chose to ignore it.

The only sign Jesus offered was the sign that when they killed Him, He would in three days rise from the dead. They had no comprehension whatsoever of what He was talking about. But Jesus was making a very real statement about TRUTH. Destroy this *NAOS*, and in three days I will raise it up! The word *naos* was the word the Lord used. It is a carefully chosen word. In the New Testament, there are two words for TEMPLE. The word *heiron* is used in some instances and the word *naos* is used in others. *Heiron* is a word used to describe the entire precinct and structure of the overall temple. That included the outer court and all that surrounded it. The word is used in Mark 11:11-27. The word *naos* on the other hand spoke of a very particular place in the overall structure of the temple. The *naos* was the sanctuary. The place where the ark of the covenant rested was the *naos*. It was the Holy of Holies. In other words, Jesus said, Destroy Fathers's HOUSE and in three days I will raise it up. The HOUSE of the Lord, as we have already discussed was the place where the Glory Cloud came down and tented the people in shade. Jesus was the *NAOS* Himself, it would release the ultimate resurrection of the *ULTIMATE NAOS*: HIS BODY, the Church, the Fullness OF HIM WHO FILLS ALL IN ALL!

In I Cor. 3:16 Paul uses the same word when he reminds the believers at Corinth that they are the *NAOS* of God. The Father had prepared a BODY For His Son (Heb. 10:15). Father's House would be a BODY, the Church, the Bride of Christ.

Remember it was zeal for Father's HOUSE that consumed Jesus. As a point of information, when the Pharisees responded to Jesus in regards to His comment about raising up a house in three days, they retort that the temple He was standing in was forty-six years in the making and still incomplete. This was a long term building project. It required a great sum of money and was all for the "glory of God". At least that was what they thought. History tells us that this temple was completed in approximately A.D. 64. Six years after its completion, in A.D. 70 it was destroyed in fulfillment of the prophecy of Jesus regarding the destruction of Jerusalem.

On the day of His crucifixion, as Jesus was fulfilling Passover in His own Body, the priests were offering up the Passover lamb in the temple. At 9:00 A.M. the knife went through the lamb of the sacrifice. So too, at nine in the morning outside the city gate on the dung heap the Lamb of God was being pierced through for our iniquities. At three in the afternoon the evening sacrifice was being laid on the alter to be slain. Except this Passover was going to be different. The fullness of times had come. God was no longer interested in externals. The inner dimension was being solidified in Christ. When the priest in the temple raised the knife to kill the evening Passover sacrifice, a voice was heard above the accusations of the mockers saying "It is FINISHED." "And behold, the veil of the *NAOS* was torn in two from top to bottom..." (Matt. 27:51). Father was no longer considering externals. No longer was Father's House inaccessible. No longer was His House off limits. No longer did the cherubim guard the way to the tree of life with a flaming sword. In actual fact that sword pierced the veil of the earthly temple and now access was available. God in Christ opened the way to the sanctuary, never again to deny access to those that believe. The veil was torn from TOP to BOTTOM. God did it! God brought the GARDEN to us in CHRIST! John 13 and 14 becomes crystal clear now. Peter was willing to follow Jesus anywhere, but Jesus said where He was going now Peter could not come but he would follow later (13:36). Jesus was to be both High Priest and Sacrifice. He was about to enter within the veil with His own blood to make atonement for the sins of not just Israel but the WHOLE WORLD! Jesus had to fulfill the Law. Peter was not yet able to have access to the *NAOS*. He would, however, follow later by virtue of the blood of Christ!

Jesus made it clear that Father's House had plenty of room for all of them. He wasn't speaking of the little ten-by-ten cube called the Holy of Holies. He was speaking of REALITY. But to bring the REAL into existence He had to fulfill the externals. He said if He went to prepare a place for them, He would come again and receive them unto

THINGS

HIMSELF. Aaron never could say that he was going to make
atonement and would come out to receive the people unto
himself. Aaron was never quite sure that once he entered
within the veil he would come out again alive. But Jesus
boldly made that claim: "I will come again and receive you
to Myself, that where I am there you may be also." (14:3).
Beloved, this is not speaking of the second coming, this is
speaking of the work that was accomplished at the first
coming. Christ came out from the veil alive and satisfying
once and for all the demands of righteousness, and thus
made room for all of us in Father's HOUSE!

We have become the very HOUSE of God. God is not
interested in temples made of hands. He is building a temple
of living stones, with an everlasting CORNERSTONE that
cannot fall. (I Peter 2:4-ff)

What is true of Christ as the Heavenly Man at the
resurrection is true of the Church. As He is, so also are we in
the Father. "Who has heard such things" Can a land be born
in a day? Can a nation be brought forth all at once? As soon
as Zion travailed she brought forth her sons!" (Isa. 66:8).
How did Zion travail! She travailed in the fullness of times
through Christ the mighty Intercessor, Who became sin on
our behalf. In three days, God raised up a nation. In that
DAY the Church was birthed in GLORY. We became sons
by His finished work.

The internal block was removed, and the inner dimension
was established "He breaks the power of cancelled sin, He
sets the Prisoner free", sang John Wesley. The CROSS of
Christ is the great divide. The CROSS accomplished something for the FATHER. It enabled the Father to invest the
fullness of His Glory in a people without hindrance. The
Last Adam had conquered. The Last Adam justified us all.
The CROSS put a gulf between the Old and the New. The
CROSS bridged the gap between the familiar and the

unfamiliar. The CROSS is the transitional point where we passed from external to internal.

Consider the words of the writer to the Hebrews:

> For You Have Not Come To A Mountain That May Be Touched And To A Blazing Fire And To Darkness And Gloom And Whirlwind...But You Have Come To Mount Zion And To The City Of The Living God, The Heavenly Jerusalem, And To Myriads Of Angels, To The General Assembly And Church Of The First-Born, Who Are Enrolled In Heaven, And To God, The Judge Of All, And To The Spirits Of Righteous Men Made Perfect, And To Jesus, The Mediator Of A New Covenant, And To The Sprinkled Blood Which Speaks Better Than The Blood Of Able. (12:18-24).

We **have** come. In Christ we have arrived. We are the people who once were not a people but now are the very people of God. Christ brought us back to the GARDEN. He restored us to God's Glory. In actual fact we are already within the veil. The writer to the Hebrews takes great pain to express that truth. Yet because of unbelief, we have put off to the future, what is ours by birthright NOW. Life within the veil is PRESENT TRUTH.

We have been brought to the MOUNTAIN of God, ZION was established as the chief of the mountains (Isa. 2:1-ff) as a result of the ascension of Christ. Christ was installed as KING at His ascension. This was the promise made to Him before the foundation of the world: "But as for Me, I have installed My King upon Zion, My holy mountain." (Psalm 2:6).

Peter attests to that truth on the Day of Pentecost when he declares:

> This Jesus, God raised up again, to which we are all witnesses. Therefore, having been EXALTED to the right hand of God, and having received from the

Father the promise of the Holy Spirit, He has poured
forth this which you both see and hear... Therefore let
all the house of Israel know for certain, that God has
made Him both Lord and Christ. (Acts 2:32-ff).

Jesus is not the coming King. He is the KING Who is
COMING. There is a world of difference. He is not waiting
to take the throne of His father David, Peter makes plain in
his sermon at Pentecost that Jesus is already on David's
Throne!

He is installed as King over the CITY of Zion. It is a
LITERAL CITY. But it is literal in the SPIRIT. Our rational
view of reality, which is not reality at all, causes us to say
that spiritual things are not as real as physical things. In
truth, however, spiritual things are far more real. For that
which is visible was made out of that which is INVISIBLE.
The only reason the material world has substance is because
it exists by the power of the invisible world, the world of the
Spirit of God.

Abraham looked for a CITY with eternal foundations.
You cannot find eternal foundations in brick and mortar.
God put eternity in the HEART of Abraham. We are never
called to look and evaluate upon the basis of those things
that are seen, but upon that which is unseen, for the unseen
is eternal, while the visible is temporary (2 Cor. 4:18).

The New Creation in Christ reveals a New Order, a New
Species and a New Temple. He comes to make all things
NEW. I believe there will ultimately one day be a new
heaven above us, and a new earth beneath our feet, but I
also believe, that since the ascension of Messiah I am living
under a New Heaven. There is a New Zion and a New
Jerusalem. Its reality is not seen with the natural, eye but
rather it is seen inwardly with the eyes of the Spirit. It
requires the impartation of eye salve by the Spirit to see the
New thing God is doing. When the prophet declares: "Behold,
I will do something NEW, NOW it will spring forth; will you

not be aware of it? (Isa.42:19)?'' We read that verse and don't
have the slightest idea of what he spoke. Isaiah saw God
ushering in a whole new order and creation in a day yet
ahead of him, and he sees it before it happens; DON'T MISS
IT. Some of us are not even aware that we are living in the
NEW DAY. The NEW DAY began at the ascension of Christ.
This is the DAY that the Lord has made!

Because we have reduced much of the Scripture to a
rational interpretation, and by rational I mean that which
we can interpret upon the basis of limited logic apart from
the revelation of the Holy Spirit, we come up with systems
of theology that constantly put off into the future what God
says is ours NOW. Men and women that are afraid to
uncover the foundations of their view of the future give the
excuse that it isn't important what you believe about the
"end times". That statement could not be further from the
truth. Your perception of what will happen in the future has
a great deal to do with how you live your life in the present.
Don't be deceived, your eschatology is vitally important to
your view of life, the world and history, and has a definite
effect upon your behavior.

If Jesus is the Alpha and the Omega, then He stands both
at the beginning and at the end of history to insure that
God's ultimate purpose will be totally fulfilled. We have
been paralyzed by anemic eschatology. A view of the end
times that places the binding of satan in the future when
Colossians plainly declares it is in the past, is an anemic
eschatology. An eschatology that places more power on
144,000 saints in the tribulation period without the aid of the
Holy Spirit, to evangelize the lost, while the Spirit all
through this present age has been doing that very thing
through the Church, is an anemic and erroneous eschatology. If the Holy Spirit is the agency by which men come to
Christ, how can it be that 144,000 so called tribulation saints
can accomplish more without Him than the Church has

been able to accomplish with Him for almost 2,000 years?

An eschatology that divides up the character and nature of God's movements into dispensations, ultimately denies that He is the same yesterday, today and forever. This too, is an anemic eschatology. God is not a DISPENSATIONALIST.

There are many fine men of God, who were revered as Church fathers, apostolic fathers if you will, down through the ages of history, holy men of God, who lived and died for Jesus that never embraced such fanciful interpretations of Holy Writ. Were these men SEDUCED by the new age movement? As you study the early Church fathers you find little about a view of history that lends itself to the almost annihilation of the Church at the end of the age. You find in the history of the Church, ascribing great power to antichrist and to the forces of darkness, so that all that remains at the appearing of Jesus is a weak little remnant fearfully hiding in a corner just hanging on until Jesus comes.

Some of our modern day evangelists are proclaiming by their zeal their own opinions when their theology falls far short of a proper Biblical hermeneutic.

Pauline escathology had very little room for a secret coming, and then many other appearings. Christ appeared ONCE for sin and will appear a second time for SALVATION. NOW is the only day of salvation.

The Work of Christ would be in vain, if God were to once again acknowledge the blood of bulls and goats in a rebuilt altar in the Middle East. It would be an abomination to God to look with favor upon such a sacrifice since the once for all sacrifice in Christ has been made.

Our view of the future makes a great difference in the way we live today. One causes men to live in fear, the other causes men to rise to their high and holy calling and OCCUPY until He comes. The word occupy means far more than take up space. It means to take charge. We need to begin preparing the generations yet to be born. They need to be prepared to walk with God regardless of what comes their way, should the Lord tarry.

God is moving us towards the FULLNESS of things. As there was a fullness of times for the first coming of Christ, so there is a fullness of times for the second coming of Christ.

> In Him, we have redemption through His blood, the forgiveness of our trespasses, according to the riches of His grace, which He lavished upon us. In all wisdom and insight He made known to us the mystery of His will, according to His kind intention which He purposed in Him, with a view to an administration suitable to the FULLNESS OF TIMES, that is THE SUMMING UP OF ALL THINGS IN CHRIST, things in the heavens and things upon the earth (Eph.1:7-10).

The appearing of the Lord in the first Advent was to bring to us the ability to live in the powers of the coming age. That age was coming even as Jesus ministered, and it is still coming. It is coming in FULLNESS. It will ultimately swallow up this age and overtake it. The earth and the heavens will be purged of every trace of sin and unrighteousness, and the tares will be removed from the wheat and the Kingdom will be delivered in fullness up to the Father by the Lord Jesus. The Scripture makes plain that He must reign until the last enemy is put under His feet. The last enemy is not Communism, nor is it secular humanism. To be sure, we need to wage spiritual warfare against these malicious enemies of the gospel, but they are not the last enemy of Christ. The last enemy is DEATH. He will bring even death under His subjection for He already has the power to do so. This He received when He rose from death, but He has withheld releasing that ultimate power until the FULLNESS OF TIMES.

Christ has already abolished death and brought life and immortality to light in the gospel (2 Timothy 1:10). He has the power to subject death to Himself, since He has already conquered. Yet He is reserving such until the FULLNESS of times. Until that time, He calls us by faith to live in the powers of the coming age as though it were already here. That is the essence and nature of faith. Faith already possesses the substance of what is to come.

Jesus asked the question, "When the Son of Man comes, will He find faith on the earth?" Are we really living the life that He died to bring us? Do we really live in the Holy of Holies, or do we choose rather to create a theology to match our low level of spiritual power? Like Martha, Jesus comes to us and says "Your brother will rise again", and we respond, "I believe in the DOCTRINE OF THE RESURRECTION. I learned in catechism class that on the last day all will be raised up, and we sing our hymns of that glorious day in the bye and bye when we'll fly like birds out of this mess." Jesus stands at the tombs of our lives and weeps over our unbelief. Jesus didn't weep for Lazarus. He wept over the unbelief of the people. Jesus said to Martha in plain language "Martha, resurrection is not a DOCTRINE. I AM THE RESURRECTION AND THE LIFE!" (John 11:20-25).

We do not really believe that we HAVE COME UNTO MOUNT ZION. It's Easier To Put Off Into The Eternal Age Or Into The Millennium What Our Unbelief Tells Us Is Not For Now. The issue is that our faith is in the wrong place. There are thieves and robbers in our temples and we don't even know it. The Lord must come to us with a whip and cleanse us of the attitudes that rob us of the substances of the age to come.

Jude closes his epistle with this benediction:

Now to Him who is able to keep you from stumbling, and make you stand in the presence of His glory BLAMELESS WITH GREAT JOY. To the Only God our Saviour, through Jesus Christ our Lord, be GLORY,

MAJESTY, DOMINION, and AUTHORITY, before all time and NOW and forever.

That is a mouthful. But much of our preaching of the gospel is intended to keep people bound in failure and sin. Much of our preaching is not the Gospel of grace that makes men arise to their level of greatness in God. It is the gospel of legalism which ministers death and condemnation and keeps them believing they are still in the outer court, and must depend upon the ministry of another to go before God on their behalf. A mere man takes their place before the throne, because they really don't have the kind of access to God that the preacher does.

We have been angered by the trappings of liturgy that present men as mediators on behalf of other men, but we ought look at the messages we preach to the sheep and see if while we condemn the practice in another denomination, our teaching produces the same result.

Our High Priest is in the True Tabernacle, ever living to make intercession for us. We can boldly approach the throne because it is a throne of GRACE, not based upon our performance, but based totally upon the finished work of Christ.

Christ bids us to live in the FULLNESS of His Presence. He bids us to walk with the Father even as He walked with the Father. It can only happen as, by faith, we possess that place of responsibility before God, where we are willing to be honest and admit where we are, finding grace to help in time of need.

Paul makes it clear that this is where God is taking us. There is a fullness we have yet to experience in our walk with God. Five-fold ministry is not an end in itself. It is important to realize that God has apostles and prophets, evangelists, pastors and teachers today in the Church. I am aware that some believe that there are no longer apostles and prophets, but that does not change the teaching of

Scripture. Tragically, there are those that teach and preach that God has given all five ministries to the Church, and yet they refuse to function in that reality, in order to see the Church come to fullness. Yet just as tragic, are those who claim to practice functioning in a five-fold concept, and yet have made five-fold ministry the end all of the purposes of God. Paul answers all those things quite clearly in Ephesians 4. He readily acknowledges that apostles and prophets are still in existence and called to lay the structural foundations for every New Testament Church (Eph. 2:20). He acknowledges that evangelists and pastors and teachers are to build on the foundations that apostolic and prophetic ministry have laid. It would be wonderful if we could say that the Church as a whole has come this far, but it hasn't. Yet we will die for the belief that "any moment now" Jesus is going to catch us all away.

Now I realize we are a bit beyond square one, but we aren't **much** farther than that. Paul makes plain that the purposes of functional, and I stress FUNCTIONAL, five-fold ministry is for the purpose of equipping the saints for the work of the ministry to the end that the BODY MIGHT BE BUILT UP. The word he uses is the "edifying" of itself. The word describes a building being built with walls and foundations. This is the New Creation Temple that is being built by the Spirit to be a HABITATION of God in the Spirit. The Church is still being built, beloved. As long as it is still being built, we don't contain the FULLNESS, YET. The Glory did not descend in fullness upon the Temple of Solomon until it was completed. Paul says that five-fold ministry is called to function such that we "ALL ATTAIN TO THE UNITY OF THE FAITH, AND THE KNOWLEDGE OF THE SON OF GOD, TO A MATURE MAN (SINGULAR), TO THE MEASURE OF THE STATURE WHICH BELONGS TO THE **FULLNESS** OF CHRIST." (4:11-13).

The unity of the faith is not where we are all going to agree on mode of baptism, nor on a doctrine of church membership. The unity of THE FAITH, is that place where we all realize our essential oneness with the Father, to the degree that it releases us from every hindrance that keeps us from fulfilling our unique destiny in the construction of the New Creation Temple. It is that place where according to our gifts and calling individually, we minister with the same freedom that Jesus had that caused Him to say, "I do nothing but what I see the Father doing" (John 5:19-ff).

The knowledge of the Son of God is not doctrinal, it is an experiential awareness that is held both individually and corporately of the Exalted Christ. It is a perfect knowledge of Him. That does not come by doctrine alone. That comes by encounter with HIM. In the New Covenant God promised "They shall ALL KNOW ME, from the least to the greatest." That is more than "knowing" the historical Jesus, and more than "knowing" the doctrinal Jesus. In essence it is the KNOWING by IMPARTATION THE INCARNATIONAL CHRIST WITHIN US. HE, the LIVING Word is to be made flesh in us in the FULLNESS of that EXPERIENCE. When all things are ultimately summed up IN CHRIST, He Who is now the HOPE AND GLORY within us, will be the SUBSTANCE OF GLORY WITHIN US.

The Mature Man is the Body of Christ in corporate expression, expressing the absolute maturity of sonship that no longer sees things in a glass darkly but sees face to face in the full light of His glory and love. Paul said that when he was a child, he spoke, acted and thought as a child, but when he became a man, a MATURE MAN, he put away all that resembled childishness and immaturity (I Cor. 13:11). Immaturity causes us to see dimly, and denies the perfect love of God to flow through us. But when we come of full age, it is when we have allowed the love of God to so work in us that we no longer see things dimly, but we become transparent before one another, for the fear of rejection has been cleansed away and PUT AWAY as immature. As perfect love casts out fear in our relationship with the Father, so it will do the same in our relationship one with another. *Perfect*love and *mature* love are the same thing. As a matter of fact, the word Paul uses for MATURE man, and the word John uses for PERFECT LOVE, are EXACTLY the same. The level of maturity and perfection God desires to bring us to in the Church, is where we see one another in the light of non-judgmental, unconditional love, that causes us to minister perfectly to the needs of each other. That is not something that causes us to wink at sin, but rather it causes us to accept people where they are and see them as they can be, and minister to them out of the heart of God. In this manner, He can bring them and us to that place of wholeness. I know that I am not there yet. Are you?

Finally, Paul talks about the measure of the stature that belongs to the fullness of Christ. Christ grew in favor stature with God and men. So too, God desires to exalt the Church to a place of honor and responsibility and authority and power. There is a fullness of stature for this new temple. There was a day when a native New Yorker thought that the fullness of stature in a building was expressed in the Empire State Building. But then someone built the World Trade Center. Beloved, it does not yet appear what we shall be. There is a FULLNESS OF STATURE for the NEW CREATION TEMPLE that has yet to be seen.

Five-fold ministry is only the scaffolding on the building. It is not the end in itself. We need to be careful how we build this New Temple, for if we build it so that people become dependent upon us, it will not endure the storms of testing. Only Christ's Preeminence in the life of the Church can survive the shakings that come, and they will continue to come. Remember, the writer to the Hebrews quoted Haggai the prophet and said that God would not only shake the earthly, but the HEAVENLY structures as well. We must therefore build on the unshakeable foundation of Christ, to insure that the edifice will endure the contrary winds that assail it. Large buildings such as the World Trade Center, or the Empire State are built to sway in the wind so that they do not crumble and fall during severe weather conditions. So too, Paul makes it clear that when we are built upon a solid foundation, and five-fold ministry foundations to achieve God's goals in the Church, we are no longer going to be children (immature), TOSSED HERE AND THERE by EVERY WIND OF DOCTRINE, AND THE TRICKERY OF MEN...(4:14).

My encounters with the Church at large show me that we are still crumbling with every new wind of doctrine, and being tossed here and there, unsure of our foundations. Christ lives to bring the Church to maturity. He is seated at the right hand of God to accomplish that end. He will not be moved from that position until all is accomplished. The heavens must receive Him UNTIL the period of the restoration of all things which was SPOKEN BY THE PROPHETS from ancient times on behalf of God (Acts 3:21). The heavens are holding Jesus until all that the prophets prophesied about the Church is brought into FULLNESS. Zion is to be preeminent above all the other mountains of the earth. It will take preeminence over ALL. The City of Zion will outlast the City of Babylon. For the King reigns on Zion, and the Father has expressly promised that Jesus will sit at His right hand until every enemy is made His footstool! (Psalm 110:1).

If this is true, how shall we conduct ourselves during our time allotted to us on the earth? Peter says we are to be

....looking for and HASTENING the coming of the day of God, on account of which the heavens will be destroyed by burning, and the elements will melt with intense heat! But according to His promise we are looking for new heavens and a new earth, in which righteousness dwells. Therefore beloved, since you look for these things, be DILIGENT, to be found in Him in PEACE, SPOTLESS AND BLAMELESS, and regard the PATIENCE OF OUR LORD TO BE SALVATION... (2 Peter 3:12-15).

Even Peter talks about patiently waiting for the FULL-NESS of times. Jesus does not require U.S. military intelligence or nuclear weaponry, or Soviet missiles to cause the earth to be consumed by fire. All He has to do is withdraw the power He has to uphold all things by His Word, and the elements will melt with white hot heat from the all-consuming fire of the Presence of His Glory. Our God is a consuming fire. He has reserved the destruction of the earth for Himself. His glory He will not share with another! The earth is not man's to destroy. The earth is the Lord's and the fullness thereof. He will allow man to go so far, and no further. He has purposed to sum all things up in Christ, not in nuclear holocaust. Beloved, your God is much greater than that. He is not limited by arms limitations agreements or nuclear test ban treaties. He sits as KING. He sat as KING at the FLOOD, HE sits as KING FOREVER (Psalm 29:10). He destroyed the earth the first time, He will purge it by fire the next time. The first destruction was external, the second will be internal. Our God reigns!

EPILOGUE

BEING DOERS OF
THE WORD

Sometimes as we consider where the Church is, and think about where it should be we can get terribly discouraged. We look and see the condition she is in and we shudder and cry out "Lord How Long?" Just like Isaiah cried out in Isaiah 6, and Habakuk cried out in the opening chapter of his prophecy. Buy God has ever called us to live by faith and not by sight. God promised that He would sum up all thins in Christ and that He would bring the Church to fullness. That is His promise, based on His Word. We know that no Word of God has ever failed. It cannot return to Him void, without accomplishing the purpose for which He caused it to proceed from His mouth.

When John the apostle was banished to the isle of Patmos things looked bleak indeed. The Church was struggling,

there were heresies being taught, and immorality being
practiced, and believers being martyred. It would be easy to
grow discouraged. He knew full well the intent of God in
this age for the Church. I am sure he wondered how long it
would take for God to fulfill His purposes. I am sure he also
wondered whether or not the Church would ever be
perfected in beauty and power. He sorely needed a word
from God. He has been exiled for his faith, they tried to boil
him in oil and that didn't work. They couldn't kill him. So
they banished him to a desolate island where rebels were
far removed from being a threat to imperial Rome.

Thank God that though man can be imprisoned, God
cannot be imprisoned. At the end of his life, John is given a
panoramic view of redemptive history from beginning to
end. He sees redemption from paradise lost to paradise
regained. And at the end of the vision the angel who is
guiding him through each visionary experience says these
words: "Come here and I will show you the BRIDE, the
WIFE of the Lamb" (Rev. 21:9). There are many pictures
and metaphors of the Church in the New Testament. Some
people have a hard time seeing them all as relating to the
same group of people, and yet they do. Some people have a
hard time correlating the metaphor of a Bride, with the
metaphor of a Body. But the only difference is in our
perspective, for each describes uniquely a place the Church
holds in relationship to God. While confined to exile, the
Word of the God came to John. He was about to see the
Bride, the Wife of the Lamb. This is how the account
continues:

And he carried me away *in the Spirit* (beloved, if we
are not allowing the Spirit to show us the truth it will
remain vague and mysterious, and the end result will
be a carnal interpretation of spiritual reality), to a great
and high MOUNTAIN (once again we see that a
MOUNTAIN is in view, and John has now come to a

MOUNTAIN), and showed me the holy CITY, (Ye have come to the CITY of the Living God —Heb.12:22), JERUSALEM COMING DOWN OUT OF HEAVEN FROM GOD (...To the Heavenly Jerusalem...Heb. 12:22), having the GLORY OF GOD...

The Lord is showing John the Bride, the Wife of the Lamb. Heaven help us to see the truth revealed here. Our carnal minds conjure up a picture of a satellite city hovering over the earth in some distant age. The Spirit expressly makes plain that this is the Church. It is the same Church that the writer to the Hebrews refers to as the MOUNTAIN and CITY of God. It is the same structure that Paul prays we would see in fullness in the book of Ephesians. He asks God to open the eyes of our heart to know the hope of His calling (Eph. 1:17). He goes on to pray that we might know the BREADTH, LENGTH, HEIGHT AND DEPTH OF THE LOVE OF CHRIST (Eph. 3:17). The angel tells John the CITY must be measured in Rev. 21:15. And he must measure the length, width and height and depth of that City. The City is a PERFECT CUBE. That is impractical for a City. But it is not so impractical if the CITY is a TEMPLE. A City is not buildings it is PEOPLE. The Temple is not brick and mortar, it is LIVING STONES. As with the temple of Solomon, no tools were heard cutting the stones at the temple site. This is not a temple made with hands. This temple is the New Creation Temple, brought into existence through Christ by the Spirit! The City measures 1500 x 1500 x 1500. All sides are equal. Other translations may say 12000 cubits by 12000 cubits by 12000 cubits. Either way it is the same measurement. Why a perfect cube? If you remember, when God dealt with externals under the Old Covenant, Moses had to make all the furnishings and the parts of the tabernacle according to the heavenly pattern. There was only one other perfect cube ever mentioned in all of Scripture. IT was the HOLY OF HOLIES where the ark of

God rested, and the GLORY dwelt. IT was 10 x 10 x 10. That was the Old Creation temple. It was small, and there was not room in it for anything except the ark of the covenant. Even the high priest was only in it once a year. But Jesus promised that in His Father's House there were MANY DWELLING PLACES. He came to build a new temple, a new holy of holies. The Church is that New Temple. We are the Holy of Holies. In the Mosaic tabernacle, there was no natural light in the Holiest of All. In the New Creation temple we are also told: "And the City has no need of the sun or of the moon to shine upon it, for the GLORY OF GOD has illumined it and its LAMP IS THE LAMB!" (21:23). There is so much in the Spirit to see here. Pray that the Lord will give you insight and revelation.

The City has twelve gates, 12 being the number of governmental perfection. It's foundation stones are apostolic ministries (Eph. 2:20) (Rev. 21:14). The walls are great and high. God says the the walls of Zion will be called SALVATION (Isa. 60:18). The writer to the Hebrews warns against neglecting SO GREAT A SALVATION (Heb. 2:3). The Gates of the City are made of Pearl. The GATES OF ZION ARE CALLED PRAISE (Isa. 60:18). It is significant that the gates are made of Pearl (Rev. 21:21) Each gate was made of a SINGLE PEARL. Pearl is the only precious stone in existence that is brought into existence by way of suffering. The oyster is caused to suffer over a grain of sand which is a foreign object that irritates the sensitive body of the oyster. The oyster secrets a fluid that coats the sand until after continual secretions it becomes hard, white and beautiful. Gates speak of entrance and access. The only way into the City of God is by faith in the SUFFERINGS OF CHRIST on our behalf. His death brought into existence the PEARL OF GREAT PRICE. It is a SINGLE PEARL. Anyone who seeks to come in any other way except the gate of Christ is a thief and a robber. There is only one way into the City of God.

John also sees the River of Life flowing out of that City
(22:1). The same way the river flowed out of Eden, now the
River of Life flows out of the restored City of God. The
allusion here is to the river that Ezekiel sees in his prophecy
(47:1-ff). Every place the river flows there is life. (Compare
Rev 22 with Ezek. 47). On either side of the River John sees
the Tree of Life bringing forth 12 kinds of fruit in every
season. The leaves of the trees are for the healing of the
nations (22:2). What a marvelous picture. Beloved, if this is
all for the millennial age there are some tremendous
problems, for there will be no need of healing in the
millennium, according to those who teach as it as such. John
goes on to say that there shall no longer be any curse.
Without a doubt the fullness of this will not be seen until He
consummates all things, but isn't it true that Christ has
already delivered us from the curse?

John goes on to talk about face to face communion with
God. He goes on to say that the NAME of God is on the
foreheads of His bondservants in that City. Beloved we hear
so much about the mark of the beast. If you are the
bondservant of Christ you have the name of God on your
forehead. Why don't we ever hear a sermon about the Name
of God written on our foreheads instead of sermons about
those that have the mark of the beast? If you care to accept
it, this, too, is a PRESENT TRUTH, not some future
experience.

John closes the letter He writes to the seven Churches of
Asia Minor by giving this exhortation: "And the Spirit and
the Bride say **COME,** and let the one who HEARS say
COME. And let the one who is thirsty **COME**; and let the one
who wishes take the water of life WITHOUT COST" (see
Isaiah 55:1). For years I glossed over these verses thinking I
knew what they said. I assumed that the Spirit and the
Bride were saying "COME" to the Lord Jesus. But the Bride
is the agency by which the Spirit calls to those outside of the

City that are thirsty and in need of life to come freely by way of the gate of Christ to partake of the Tree of Life and be healed. Outside the city are the sorcerers and dogs, and immoral of this world, but also outside according to 22:14-15 are those that see their need and desire to wash their garments that they might have access to the TREE OF LIFE in the midst of the City.

What a tremendous way to close the last book of the Bible, with an invitation to partake of FULLNESS of LIFE in the City of God. John saw the Church by the Spirit in all its fullness. We are called to offer the call to those outside that are in need to come and partake. There yet remains a FULLNESS that the Church will experience. John saw it at a distance and welcomed it. Jesus testified of it and said in closing that He was indeed coming quickly to fulfill it! What shall we say then? I believe the only response we can make is the same response that John made when Jesus said, "Yes, I am coming quickly" (22:20). We must add our Amen to John's Amen. Let us realize that to Jesus "quickly" is not time and space limited. The Lord is not slow regarding His promise. He is coming in a moment and in the twinkling of an eye to JOIN HIS BRIDE IN FULLNESS. Together they shall reign unhindered over all the earth, and the universe as vast as it is. Beloved, the BEST IS YET TO COME. AMEN! COME LORD JESUS!

Mark J. Chironna

Have you crossed the Jordan?

THE ELISHA PRINCIPLE is for those of you who are serious about going on with God. Explored in this selection are the consequences of disobedience versus the fruits of obedience.

We have all experienced our own particular "Jordan": those places where we must overtly choose to obey or disobey the voice of God. Are we willing to "jump in" and trust Him? Do we tentatively "wade" to test the water and jump back out again...? What do YOU do?

Between these covers you will discover thought-provoking dissertation, enthusiastic discourse and renewed vision!

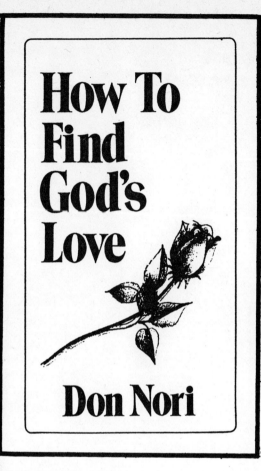

**Significant New
Witnessing Tool
for our
Generation**

Retail $2.95

Help lead others to the Lord Jesus! For Evangelistic
purposes. Packets of 10 — $2.00 each includes postage.

Packets of 20 Books— $1.50 each includes postage.

- 96 Page Book
- Significant Testimonies
- Genuinely leads people to Christ

Prophetic Books
──────International──────

Prophetic Books International offers many significant prophetic titles for this generation. For a free catalog listing these titles please write to:

P.B.I.
P.O. Box 351
Shippensburg, PA 17257